The West Country Book

Foreword by
H.R.H. The Prince of Wales, Duke of Cornwall

Edited and with an Introduction by
J.C. Trewin

Webb&Bower
EXETER, ENGLAND

First published in Great Britain 1981 by
Webb & Bower (Publishers) Limited
33 Southernhay East, Exeter, Devon

Designed by Giolitto Wrigley & Couch Design Partnership
24a Gandy Street, Exeter, Devon

British Library Cataloguing in Publication Data
The West Country book.
1. English literature—England—West Country
2. English literature—20th century
I. Trewin, John Courtenay
820'.8'09423   PR8389.W
ISBN 0-906671-23-X

Printed and bound in the West Country by A. Wheaton and
Company Limited, Exeter, Devon

Typeset by Bristol and West Engravers Limited, Bristol

Colour separation by Colthouse Repro Limited, Bournemouth

Paper made by
Reed and Smith Limited, Silverton Mills, Devon

Contents

BUCKINGHAM PALACE

While I cannot claim to be a West Country man by birth I certainly became one at a very early age, when I became Duke of Cornwall. Since that time I have grown to love that particular part of the country and its people and now I am delighted to have become *almost* a West Country man by residence.

For those who visit the area as well as the lucky people who live there and have it in their blood, Mr Trewin's book provides a splendid collection of some of the best writing on the West Country. It catches the atmosphere as it was, and still is – even if you have not been to Mousehole, Minehead or the Manacles.

I am particularly pleased that the proceeds of this book will be given to the Exeter Cathedral Preservation Trust, of which I am proud to be the President. It is one of the finest monuments to man's artistry and inspiration in the West Country and I very much hope that this book will indeed help to contribute towards its preservation.

Introduction

It is right that a book of homage to the West Country should have its heart in Exeter.

There the city's heart is the Cathedral of St Peter. Only to see its twin Norman towers governing their hill, in that flashing glimpse from the train, is to evoke the march of nave and vaulting, 'the blaze, the splendour, and the symmetry' that face all who pass through the Cathedral's western door. Today the external fabric is under repair. Hence, as the publishers' contribution to the appeal fund, this new *West Country Book* that H.R.H. the Prince of Wales, Duke of Cornwall, President of the Cathedral Preservation Trust, has graciously introduced.

Three decades ago, in another anthology based then on *The West Country Magazine* that for six years I had the honour of editing, Ivor Brown—from Buchan, in Scotland's north-east—wrote of 'the magic in the word West and in all the vision and aroma that it brings'. To everyone, of course, a different vision: the rhythms of Dartmoor; a Somerset water-and-willowscape; the southern sea in tumult against Old Lizard Head; Hardy's Egdon; the strange tangle of the Undercliff; or what Naomi Royde-Smith, one of many celebrants of the Western province, recalled as her distant view of Exeter, 'shining like old and rosy mother-of-pearl in the light of the winter afternoon', and the Cathedral 'oddly like pictures of a Chinese fortress . . . with its umbrella-topped turrets, their little pennons all flying back as in a perennial wind.'

So many writers, native or adopted, have spoken for the West: name upon name splendidly various. Some of the most distinguished, classical or contemporary, are in this book. We can remember as well—reading any literary map—that Keats ('the crystal poet leaning on the old sea-rail' of Charles Causley's phrase) completed *Endymion* at Teignmouth; that Coleridge (born at Ottery St Mary) was fatally interrupted by a person from Porlock while writing *Kubla Khan* at Ash Farm; that T.S. Eliot is buried in East Coker, Somerset; Sydney Smith, ('One of the greatest pleasures in life is conversation'), was rector of Combe Florey; Kenneth Grahame was married at Fowey which lives in *The Wind in the Willows*; D.H. Lawrence, in the middle of World War I, stayed at Zennor; Sir John Squire (with his Devon river-poem, 'the Lowman in spring, with the lent-lilies'), and L.A.G. Strong were Plymothians; Robert Herrick wrote most of his poetry in the Devon village of Dean Prior where he was vicar; Anne Treneer, Cornish of the Cornish, honoured her native Gorran; R.D. Blackmore means *Lorna Doone*, and Charles Kingsley *Westward Ho!*

The Powys brothers were Dorset-bred; William Browne, of Tavistock, called Devon, 'the blessed plot whose equal all the world affordeth not'; Henry Newbolt, once a Clifton schoolboy, is buried at Orchardleigh; Cecil Day Lewis, educated at Sherborne, lived for a time at Cheltenham and was buried at Stinsford; and, from exile, James Elroy Flecker's heart turned,

> where no sun burns
> To lands of glittering rain,
> To fields beneath low-clouded skies
> New-widowed of their grain.

The stage also. John Ford, the Jacobean dramatist (*Perkin Warbeck*), was born at Ilsington on the edge of Dartmoor; *The Fair Maid of the West* is Thomas Heywood's; Edmund Kean, at the time among the wilder pomping folk, was engaged early in 1812 to 'act every thing' in the company of the Exeter Theatre; besides the prolonged grandeur of *The Dynasts,* Hardy wrote the lesser-known *Famous Tragedy of the Queen of Cornwall* ('a tragedy of dire duresse/That vexed the land of Lyonesse'); Shaw who on occasion, worked—and swam—at Cadgwith and Mevagissey, set *You Never Can Tell* at 'a watering place on the coast of Torbay in Devon'; Eden Phillpotts—joined on occasion by his daughter Adelaide—evolved the sequence of Devon folk-comedies.

We can summon a few more names, visitors or natives. Thus Celia Fiennes, that resolute traveller (and unpunctuated writer), applauds Exeter in these terms on her journey in 1698: 'A town very well built the streetes are well pitch'd spacious noble streetes and a vast trade is carryd on . . . This Citty does exceedingly resemble London.' Alfred Tennyson, a century and a half later, sits on Kynance beach watching 'the glorious grass-green monsters of waves'. Robert Stephen Hawker walks his parish of Morwenstow in a brimless hat, a claret-coloured tail-coat over a fisherman's jersey and waders. Wilkie Collins in *Rambles Beyond Railways* sees the drama of *The Curate's Daughter* in the Sans Pareil fit-up at Redruth; Hardy, again, goes to the funeral of his friend, the Dorset dialect poet, William Barnes, at Winterborne Came and, in his poem of 'The Last Signal', records the strange sun-flash from the coffin. Less expected entrants, too: John Galsworthy (who had an ancestral Devon link) spent many summers at Manaton. Rudyard Kipling (he was at school in Westward Ho!) lived for some months in 1896-7 at Rock House, Maidencombe, working on the Stalky stories and saying to his cousin, Florence Macdonald, 'Come on, Florence, what shall we make them do now?' Parson Woodforde, of the eighteenth-century Norfolk village journal, was born at Ansford in Somerset where his journal actually begins.

'Whither should they come?' asks a Shakespearian character, and the reply is briefly, 'Up.' In this book now we thank those who have come up from the past: Jane Austen, Agatha Christie, Caroline Fox, Thomas Hardy, Frank Mansell, Sean O'Casey, Eden Phillpotts, John Prince, Sir Arthur Quiller-Couch ('Q'), William Makepeace Thackeray, Dylan Thomas (who was married at Penzance and spent his honeymoon in West Cornwall), Evelyn Waugh, Henry Williamson. From the present we thank Sir John Betjeman, Charles Causley, Dame Daphne du Maurier, John Fowles, Christopher Fry, Winston Graham, W.G. Hoskins, Laurie Lee, A.L. Rowse, Derek Tangye and Colin Wilson.

Moreover, we are grateful to many of our contemporary contributors for helping in the choice of illustrations. To everyone (I repeat) a personal vision; here we have a mosaic of the province in all its diverse splendours, cliff and moor and pasture, village, town and harbour:

> Ah! what a luxury of landscape meets
> My gaze! Proud towers, and cots more dear to me,
> Elm-shadow'd fields, and prospect-bounding sea.

That was Coleridge nearly two hundred years ago. Today he would have joined our homage to the shining West.

J.C.T.

JOHN BETJEMAN

Exeter

Sir John Betjeman, who in 1972 succeeded Cecil Day Lewis as Poet Laureate, has loved the West Country since early schoolboy holidays in Cornwall. His second book, *Continual Dew* (1937), containing *Exeter*, has the poem on Dorset that begins 'Rime Intrinseca, Fontmell Magna, Sturminster Newton and Melbury Bubb'. *Trebetherick* (in *Old Lights for New Chancels*, 1940) was his first celebration of the north coast of Cornwall; several later poems included *North Coast Recollections*, originally printed in the *West Country Magazine* (1947) and republished in the first *West Country Book* (1949). There are extended Cornish passages in the fourth and eighth chapters of the autobiography in blank verse, *Summoned by Bells* (1960).

The doctor's intellectual wife
  Sat under the ilex tree
The Cathedral bells pealed over the wall
  But never a bell heard she
And the sun played shadowgraphs on her book
  Which was writ by A. Huxléy.

Once those bells, those Exeter bells
  Called her to praise and pray
By pink, acacia-shaded walls
  Several times a day
To Wulfric's altar and riddel posts
  While the choir sang Stanford in A.

The doctor jumps in his Morris car,
  The surgery door goes bang,
Clash and whirr down Colleton Crescent,
  Other cars all go hang
My little bus is enough for us—
  Till a tram-car bell went clang.

They brought him in by the big front door
  And a smiling corpse was he;
On the dining-room table they laid him out
  Where the *Bystanders* used to be—
The Tatler, *The Sketch* and *The Bystander*
  For the canons' wives to see.

Now those bells, those Exeter bells
  Call her to praise and pray
By pink, acacia-shaded walls
  Several times a day
To Wulfric's altar and riddel posts
  And the choir sings Stanford in A.

THOMAS HARDY

The
Cliff Without
a Name

From *A Pair of Blue Eyes* (1873) by Thomas Hardy (1840-1928). Elfride Swancourt and Henry Knight are walking on the north Cornish coast. Though the height of the Cliff Without a Name is comparable with Beeny Cliff, most of the other features seem to be from Pentargan, further to the south.*

They walked along in company, sometimes with the brook between them—for it was no wider than a man's stride—sometimes close together. The green carpet grew swampy, and they kept higher up.

One of the two ridges between which they walked dwindled lower and became insignificant. That on the right hand rose with their advance, and terminated in a clearly defined edge against the light, as if it were abruptly sawn off. A little further, and the bed of the rivulet ended in the same fashion.

They had come to a bank breast-high, and over it the valley was no longer to be seen. It was withdrawn cleanly and completely. In its place was sky and boundless atmosphere; and perpendicularly down beneath them—small and far off—lay the corrugated surface of the Atlantic.

*Denys Kay-Robinson *Hardy's Wessex Re-appraised* noted in *Young Thomas Hardy* by Robert Gittings.

The small stream here found its death. Running over the precipice, it was dispersed in spray before it was half-way down, and falling like rain upon projecting ledges, made minute grassy meadows of them. At the bottom the water-drops soaked away amid the débris of the cliff. This was the inglorious end of the river . . .

'There is more to see alongside us, after all,' said Knight.

She turned . . . and saw, towering still higher than themselves, the vertical face of the hill on the right, which did not project seaward so far as the bed of the valley, but formed the back of a small bay, and so was visible like a concave wall, bending round from their position towards the left.

The composition of the huge hill was revealed to its backbone and marrow here at its rent extremity. It consisted of a vast stratification of blackish-grey slate, unvaried in its whole height by a single change of shade.

It is with cliffs and mountains as with persons; they have what is called a presence, which is not necessarily proportionate to their actual bulk. A little cliff will impress you powerfully; a great one not at all. It depends, as with man, upon the countenance of the cliff.

'I cannot bear to look at that cliff,' said Elfride. 'It has a horrid personality, and makes me shudder. We will go.'

'Can you climb?' said Knight. 'If so, we will ascend by that path over the grim old fellow's brow.'

'Try me,' said Elfride disdainfully. 'I have ascended steeper slopes than that.'

From where they had been loitering, a grassy path wound along inside a bank, placed as a safeguard for unwary pedestrians, to the top of the precipice, and over it along the hill in an inland direction . . . Reaching the very top, they sat down to rest by mutual consent.

'Heavens, what an altitude!' said Knight between his pants, and looking far over the sea. The cascade at the bottom of the slope appeared a mere span in height from where they were now . . .

'Over that edge,' said Knight, 'where nothing but vacancy appears, is a moving compact mass. The wind strikes the face of the rock, runs up it, rises like a fountain to a height far above our heads, curls over us in an arch, and disperses behind us. In fact, an inverted cascade is there—as perfect as the Niagara Falls—but rising instead of falling, and air instead of water. Now look here.'

Knight threw a stone over the bank, aiming it as if to go onward over the cliff. Reaching the verge, it towered into the air like a bird, turned back, and alighted on the ground behind them. They themselves were in a dead calm.

'A boat crosses Niagara immediately at the foot of the falls, where the water is quite still, the fallen mass curving under it. We are in precisely the same position with regard to our atmospheric cataract here. If you run back from the cliff fifty yards, you will be in a brisk wind. Now I daresay over the bank is a little backward current.'

Knight rose and leant over the bank. No sooner was his head above it than his hat appeared to be sucked from his head—slipping over his forehead in a seaward direction.

'That's the backward eddy, as I told you,' he cried, and vanished over the little bank after his hat.

Elfride waited one minute; he did not return. She waited another, and there was no sign of him.

A few drops of rain fell, then a sudden shower.

She arose, and looked over the bank. On the other side were a yard or two of level ground—then a short steep preparatory slope—then the verge of the precipice.

On the slope was Knight, his hat on his head. He was on his hands and knees, trying to climb back to the level ground. The rain had wetted the shaly surface of the incline. A slight superficial wetting of the soil hereabout made it far more slippery to stand on than the same soil thoroughly drenched. The inner substance was still hard, and was lubricated by the moistened film.

'I find a difficulty in getting back,' said Knight.

Elfride's heart fell like lead.

'But you can get back?' she wildly inquired.

Knight strove with all his might for two or three minutes, and the drops of perspiration began to bead on his brow.

'No, I am unable to do it,' he answered.

Elfride, by a wrench of thought, forced away from her mind the sensation that Knight was in bodily danger. But attempt to help him she must. She ventured upon the treacherous incline, propped herself with the closed telescope, and gave him her hand before he saw her movements.

'O Elfride! why did you?' said he. 'I am afraid you have only endangered yourself.'

And as if to prove his statement, in making an endeavour by her assistance they both slipped lower, and then he was again stayed. His foot was propped by a bracket of quartz rock, standing out like a tooth from the verge of the precipice. Fixed by this, he steadied her, her head being about a foot below the beginning of the slope. Elfride had dropped the glass; it rolled to the edge and vanished over it into a nether sky.

'Hold tightly to me,' he said.

She flung her arms round his neck with such a firm grasp that whilst he remained it was impossible for her to fall.

'Don't be flurried,' Knight continued. 'So long as we stay above this block we are perfectly safe. Wait a moment whilst I consider what we had better do.'

He turned his eyes to the dizzy depths beneath them, and surveyed the position of affairs.

Two glances told him a tale with ghastly distinctness. It was that, unless they performed their feat of getting up the slope with the precision of machines, they were over the edge and whirling in mid-air.

For this purpose it was necessary that he should recover the breath and strength which his previous efforts had cost him. So he still waited, and looked in the face of the enemy.

The crest of this terrible natural façade passed among the neighbouring inhabitants as being seven hundred feet above the water it overhung. It had been proved by actual measurement to be not a foot less than six hundred and fifty.

That is to say, it is nearly three times the height of Flamborough, half as high again as the South Foreland, a hundred feet higher than Beachy Head—the loftiest promontory on the east or south side of this island—twice the height of St Aldhelm's, thrice as high as the Lizard, and just double the height of St Bee's. One sea-bord point on the western coast is known to surpass it in altitude, but only by a few feet. This is Great Orme's Head in Caernarvonshire.

And it must be remembered that the cliff exhibits an intensifying feature which some of those are without—sheer perpendicularity from the half-tide level.

Yet this remarkable rampart forms no headland: it rather walls in an inlet—the promontory on each side being much lower. Thus, far from being salient, the horizontal section is concave. The sea, rolling direct from the shores of North America, has in fact eaten a chasm into the middle of a hill, and the giant, embayed and unobtrusive, stands in the rear of pigmy supporters. Not least singularly, neither hill, chasm, nor precipice has a name. On this account I will call the precipice the Cliff Without a Name.

What gave an added terror to its height was its blackness. And upon this dark face the beating of ten thousand west winds had formed a kind of bloom, which had a visual effect not unlike that of a Hambro' grape. Moreover it seemed to float off into the atmosphere, and inspire terror through the lungs.

'This piece of quartz, supporting my feet, is on the very nose of the cliff,' said Knight, breaking the silence after his rigid stoical meditation. 'Now what you are to do is this. Clamber up my body till your feet are on my shoulders; when you are there you will, I think, be able to climb on to level ground.'

'What will you do?'

'Wait whilst you run for assistance.'

'I ought to have done that in the first place, ought I not?'

'I was in the act of slipping, and should have reached no stand-point without your weight, in all probability. But don't let us talk. Be brave, Elfride, and climb.'

She prepared to ascend . . . 'Now put your foot into my hand: next the other. That's good—well done. Hold to my shoulder.'

She placed her feet upon the stirrup he made of his hand, and was high enough to get a view of the natural surface of the hill over the bank.

'Can you now climb on to level ground?'

'I am afraid not. I will try.'

'What can you see?'

'The sloping common.'

'What upon it?'

'Purple heather and some grass.'

'Nothing more—no man or human being of any kind?'

'Nobody.'

'Now try to get higher in this way. You see that tuft of sea-pink above you. Get that well into your hand, but don't trust to it entirely. Then step upon my shoulder, and I think you will reach the top.'

With trembling limbs she did exactly as he told her. The preternatural quiet and solemnity of his manner overspread upon herself and gave her a courage not her own. She made a spring from the top of his shoulder, and was up.

Then she turned to look at him.

By an ill fate, the force downwards of her bound, added to his own weight, had been too much for the block of quartz upon which his feet depended. It was, indeed, originally an igneous protrusion into the enormous masses of black strata, which had since been worn away from the sides of the alien fragment by centuries of frost and rain, and now left it without much support.

It moved. Knight seized a tuft of sea-pink with each hand.

The quartz rock which had been his salvation was worse than useless now. It rolled over, out of sight, and away into the same nether sky that had engulfed the telescope.

One of the tufts by which he held came out at the root, and Knight began to follow the quartz. It was a terrible moment. Elfride uttered a low wild wail of agony, bowed her head, and covered her face with her hands.

Between the turf-covered slope and the gigantic perpendicular rock intervened a weather-worn series of jagged edges, forming a face yet steeper than the former slope. As he slowly slid inch by inch upon these, Knight made a last desperate dash at the lowest tuft of vegetation—the last outlying knot of starved herbage ere the rock appeared in all its bareness. It arrested his further descent. Knight was now literally suspended by his arms; but the incline of the brow being what engineers would call about a third in one, it was sufficient to relieve his arms of a portion of the weight, but was very far from offering an adequately flat face to support him.

In spite of this dreadful tension of body and mind, Knight found time for a moment of thankfulness. Elfride was safe.

She lay on her side above him—her fingers clasped. Seeing him again steady, she jumped upon her feet.

'Now, if I can only save you by running for help!' she cried. 'Oh, I would have died instead! Why did you try so hard to deliver me?' And she turned away wildly to run for assistance.

'Elfride, how long will it take you to run to Endelstow and back?'

'Three-quarters of an hour.'

'That won't do; my hands will not hold out ten minutes. And is there nobody nearer?'

'No; unless a chance passer may happen to be.'

'He would have nothing with him that could save me. Is there a pole or stick of any kind on the common?'

She gazed around. The common was bare of everything but heather and grass.

A minute—perhaps more time—was passed in mute thought by both. On a sudden the blank and helpless agony left her face. She vanished over the bank from his sight.

Knight felt himself in the presence of a personalised loneliness. Haggard cliffs, of every ugly altitude, are as common as sea-fowl along the line of coast between Exmoor and Land's End; but this outflanked and encompassed specimen was the ugliest of them all. Their summits are not safe places for scientific experiment on the principles of air-currents, as Knight had now found, to his dismay.

He still clutched the face of the escarpment—not with the frenzied hold of despair, but with a dogged determination to make the most of his every jot of endurance, and so give the longest possible scope to Elfride's intentions, whatever they might be.

He reclined hand in hand with the world in its infancy. Not a blade, not an insect, which spoke of the present, was between him and the past. The inveterate antagonism of these black precipices to all strugglers for life is in no way more forcibly suggested than by the paucity of tufts of grass, lichens, or confervae on their outermost ledges.

Knight pondered on the meaning of Elfride's hasty disappearance, but could not avoid an instinctive conclusion that there existed but a doubtful hope for him. As far as he could judge, his sole chance of deliverance lay in the possibility of a rope or pole being brought; and this possibility was remote indeed. The soil upon these high downs was left so untended that they were unenclosed for miles, except by a casual bank or dry wall, and were rarely visited but for the purpose of collecting or counting the flock which found a scanty means of subsistence thereon.

At first, when death appeared improbable because it had never visited him before, Knight could think of no future, nor of anything connected with his past. He could only look sternly at

Nature's treacherous attempt to put an end to him, and strive to thwart her.

From the fact that the cliff formed the inner face of the segment of a huge cylinder, having the sky for a top and the sea for a bottom, which enclosed the cove to the extent of more than a semi-circle, he could see the vertical face curving round on each side of him. He looked far down the facade, and realised more thoroughly how it threatened him. Grimness was in every feature, and to its very bowels the inimical shape was desolation.

By one of those familiar conjunctions of things wherewith the inanimate world baits the mind of man when he pauses in moments of suspense, opposite Knight's eyes was an imbedded fossil, standing forth in low relief from the rock. It was a creature with eyes. The eyes, dead and turned to stone, were even now regarding him. It was one of the early crustaceans called Trilobites. Separated by millions of years in their lives, Knight and this underling seemed to have met in their place of death. It was the single instance within reach of his vision of anything that had ever been alive and had a body to save, as he himself had now.

The creature represented but a low type of animal existence, for never in their vernal years had the plains indicated by those numberless slaty layers been traversed by an intelligence worthy of the name. Zoophytes, mollusca, shell-fish, were the highest developments of those ancient dates. The immense lapses of time each formation represented had known nothing of the dignity of man. They were grand times, but they were mean times too, and mean were their relics. He was to be with the small in his death.

Knight was a fair geologist; and such is the supremacy of habit over occasion, as a pioneer of the thoughts of man, that at this dreadful juncture his mind found time to take in, by a momentary sweep, the varied scenes that had had their day between this creature's epoch and his own. There is no place like a cleft land-scape for bringing home such imaginings as these.

Time closed up like a fan before him. He saw himself at one extremity of the years, face to face with the beginning and all the intermediate centuries simultaneously. Fierce men, clothed in the hides of beasts, and carrying, for defence and attack, huge clubs and pointed spears, rose from this rock like the phantoms before the doomed Macbeth. They lived in hollows, woods, and

mud huts—perhaps in caves of the neighbouring rocks. Behind
them stood an earlier band. No man was there. Huge elephantine
forms, the mastodon, the hippopotamus, the tapir, antelopes of
monstrous size, the megatherium, and the myledon—all, for the
moment, in juxtaposition. Further back, and overlapped by these,
were perched huge-billed birds and swinish creatures as large as
horses. Still more shadowy were the sinister crocodilian outlines—
alligators and other uncouth shapes, culminating in the colossal
lizard, the iguanodon. Folded behind were dragon forms and
clouds of flying reptiles; still underneath were fishy beings of lower
development; and so on, till the lifetime scenes of the fossil
confronting him were a present and modern condition of things.
These images passed before Knight's inner eye in less than half a
minute, and he was again considering the actual present. Was he
to die? . . . He had hoped for deliverance, but what could a girl
do? He dared not move an inch. Was Death really stretching out
his hand? The previous sensation, that it was improbable he would
die, was fainter now.

However, Knight still clung to the cliff . . . New tortures
followed. The rain increased, and persecuted him with an excep-
tional persistency which he was moved to believe owed its cause
to the fact that he was in such a wretched state already. An entirely
new order of things could be observed in this introduction of rain
upon the scene. It rained upwards instead of down. The strong
ascending air carried the rain-drops with it in its race up the
escarpment, coming to him with such velocity that they stuck
into his flesh like cold needles. Each drop was virtually a shaft,
and it pierced him to his skin. The water-shafts seemed to lift
him on their points: no downward rain ever had such a torturing
effect. In a brief space he was drenched, except in two places.
These were on the top of his shoulders and on the crown of his hat.

The wind, though not intense in other situations, was strong
here. It tugged at his coat and lifted it. We are mostly accustomed
to look upon all opposition which is not animate as that of the
stolid, inexorable hand of indifference, which wears out the
patience more than the strength. Here, at any rate, hostility did
not assume that slow and sickening form. It was a cosmic agency,
active, lashing, eager for conquest: determination; not an insensate
standing in the way.

Knight had over-estimated the strength of his hands. They were getting weak already. 'She will never come again; she has been gone ten minutes,' he said to himself.

This mistake arose from the unusual compression of his experiences just now: she had really been gone but three.

'As many more minutes will be my end,' he thought.

Next came another instance of the incapacity of the mind to make comparisons at such times.

'This is a summer afternoon,' he said, 'and there can never have been such a heavy and cold rain on a summer day in my life before.'

He was again mistaken. The rain was quite ordinary in quantity; the air in temperature. It was, as is usual, the menacing attitude in which they approached him that magnified their powers.

He again looked straight downwards, the wind and the water-dashes lifting his moustache, scudding up his cheeks, under his eyelids, and into his eyes. This is what he saw down there: the surface of the sea—visually just past his toes, and under his feet; actually one-eighth of a mile, or more than two hundred yards, below them. We colour according to our moods the objects we survey. The sea would have been a deep neutral blue had happier auspices attended the gazer: it was now no otherwise than distinctly black to his vision. The narrow white border was foam, he knew well; but its boisterous tosses were so distant as to appear a pulsation only, and its plashing was barely audible. A white border to a black sea—his funeral pall and its edging.

The world was to some extent turned upside down for him. Rain descended from below. Beneath his feet was aerial space and the unknown; above him was the firm, familiar ground, and upon it all that he loved best.

Pitiless nature had then two voices, and two only. The nearer was the voice of the wind in his ears rising and falling as it mauled and thrust him hard or softly. The second and distant one was the moan of that unplummetted ocean below and afar—rubbing its restless flank against the Cliff Without a Name . . .

Nobody would have expected the sun to shine on such an evening as this. Yet it appeared, low down upon the sea. Not with its natural golden fringe, sweeping the furthest ends of the land-scape, not with the strange glare of whiteness which it sometimes puts on as an alternative to colour, but as a splotch of vermilion red upon a leaden ground—a red face looking on with a drunken leer . . .

Knight gave up thoughts of life utterly and entirely, and turned to contemplate the Dark Valley and the unknown future beyond . . . At that moment . . . something disturbed the outline of the bank above him. A spot appeared. It was the head of Elfride.

Knight immediately appeared to welcome life again . . .

Elfride had come back. What she had come to do he did not know. She could only look on at his death, perhaps. Still, she had come back, and not deserted him utterly, and it was much . . .

'How much longer can you wait?' came from her pale lips and along the wind to his position.

'Four minutes,' said Knight in a weaker voice than her own.

'But with a good hope of being saved?'

'Seven or eight.'

He now noticed that in her arms she bore a bundle of white linen, and that her form was singularly attenuated. So preter-naturally thin and flexible was Elfride at this moment that she appeared to bend under the light blows of the rain-shafts, as they struck into her sides and bosom, and splintered into spray on her face. There is nothing like a thorough drenching for reducing the protuberances of clothes, but Elfride's seemed to cling to her like a glove.

Without heeding the attack of the clouds further than by raising her hand and wiping away the spirts of rain when they went more particularly into her eyes, she sat down and hurriedly began rending the linen into strips. These she knotted end to end, and afterwards twisted them like the strands of a cord. In a short space of time she had formed a perfect rope by this means, six or seven yards long.

'Can you wait while I bind it?' she said, anxiously extending her gaze down to him.

'Yes, if not very long. Hope has given me a wonderful instalment of strength.'

Elfride dropped her eyes again, tore the remaining material into narrow tape-like ligaments, knotted each to each as before, but on a smaller scale, and wound the lengthy string she had thus formed round and round the linen rope, which, without this binding, had a tendency to spread abroad.

'Now,' said Knight . . . 'I can hold three minutes longer yet. And do you use the time in testing the strength of the knots, one by one.'

She at once obeyed, tested each singly by putting her foot on the rope between each knot, and pulling with her hands. One of the knots slipped.

'Oh, think! It would have broken, but for your forethought,' Elfride exclaimed apprehensively.

She retied the two ends. The rope was now firm in every part.

'When you have let it down,' said Knight, already resuming his position of ruling power, 'go back from the edge of the slope, and over the bank as far as the rope will allow you. Then lean down, and hold the end with both hands.'

He had first thought of a safer plan for his own deliverance, but it involved the disadvantage of possibly endangering her life.

'I have tied it round my waist,' she cried, 'and I will lean directly upon the bank, holding with my hands as well.'

It was the arrangement he had thought of, but would not suggest.

'I will raise and drop it three times when I am behind the bank,' she continued, 'to signify that I am ready. Take care, O, take the greatest care, I beg you!'

She dropped the rope over him, to learn how much of its length it would be necessary to expend on that side of the bank, went back, and disappeared as she had done before.

The rope was trailing by Knight's shoulders. In a few moments it twitched three times.

He waited yet a second or two, then laid hold.

The incline of this upper portion of the precipice, to the length only of a few feet, useless to a climber empty-handed, was invaluable now. Not more than half his weight depended entirely on the linen rope. Half a dozen extensions of the arms, alternating with half a dozen seizures of the rope with his feet, brought him up to the level of the soil.

He was saved, and by Elfride.

He extended his cramped limbs like an awakened sleeper, and sprang over the bank.

At sight of him she leapt to her feet with almost a shriek of joy . . . Moved by an impulse neither could resist, they ran together and into each other's arms . . .

She seemed as small as an infant. He perceived whence she had obtained the rope . . . The door had been made upon a woman's wit, and it had found the way out. Behind the bank, whilst Knight reclined upon the dizzy slope waiting for death, she had taken off her whole clothing, and replaced only her outer bodice and skirt. Every thread of the remainder lay upon the ground in the form of a woollen and cotton rope.

'I am used to being wet through,' she said. 'I have been drenched on Pansy dozens of times. Goodbye till we meet, clothed and in our right minds, by the fireside at home.'

She then ran off from him through the pelting rain like a hare; or more like a pheasant when, scampering away with a lowered tail, it has a mind to fly, but does not. Elfride was soon out of sight.

LAURIE LEE

Winter and Summer

Two pictures from *Cider With Rosie* (1959) of early boyhood in a Cotswold village. Besides his sensitive poetry, Laurie Lee has written the acclaimed *As I Walked Out One Midsummer Morning* (1969) and much else.

Towards Christmas there was heavy snow, which raised the roads to the tops of the hedges. There were millions of tons of the lovely stuff, plastic, pure, all-purpose, which nobody owned, which one could carve or tunnel, eat, or just throw about. It covered the hills and cut off the villages, but nobody thought of rescues; for there was hay in the barns and flour in the kitchens, the women baked bread, the cattle were fed and sheltered—we'd been cut off before, after all.

The week before Christmas, when snow seemed to lie thickest, was the moment for carol-singing; and when I think back to those nights it is to the crunch of snow and to the lights of the lanterns on it. Carol-singing in my village was a special tithe for the boys, the girls had little to do with it. Like hay-making, blackberrying, stone-clearing, and wishing-people-a-happy-Easter, it was one of our seasonal perks.

By instinct we knew just when to begin it; a day too soon and we should have been unwelcome, a day too late and we should have received lean looks from people whose bounty was already exhausted. When the true moment came, exactly balanced, we recognised it and were ready.

So as soon as the wood had been stacked in the oven to dry for the morning fire, we put on our scarves and went out through the streets, calling loudly between our hands, till the various boys who knew the signal ran out from their houses to join us.

One by one they came stumbling over the snow, swinging their lanterns round their heads, shouting and coughing horribly.

'Coming carol-barking then?'

We were the Church Choir, so no answer was necessary. For a year we had praised the Lord out of key, and as a reward for this service—on top of the Outing—we now had the right to visit all the big houses, to sing our carols and collect our tribute.

To work them all in meant a five-mile foot journey over wild and generally snowed-up country. So the first thing we did was to plan our route; a formality, as the route never changed. All the same, we blew on our fingers and argued; and then we chose our Leader. This was not binding, for we all fancied ourselves as Leaders, and he who started the night in that position usually trailed home with a bloody nose.

Eight of us set out that night. There was Sixpence the Tanner, who had never sung in his life (he just worked his mouth in church); the brothers Horace and Boney, who were always fighting everybody and always getting the worst of it; Clergy Green, the preaching maniac; Walt the bully, and my two brothers. As we went down the lane other boys, from other villages, were already about the hills, bawling 'Kingwenslush', and shouting through keyholes 'Knock on the knocker! Ring at the Bell! Give us a penny for singing so well!' They weren't an approved charity as we were, the Choir; but competition was in the air.

Our first call as usual was the house of the Squire, and we trooped nervously down his drive. For light we had candles in marmalade-jars suspended on loops of string, and they threw pale gleams on the towering snowdrifts that stood on each side of the drive. A blizzard was blowing, but we were well wrapped up, with Army puttees on our legs, woollen hats on our heads, and several scarves around our ears.

As we approached the Big House across its white silent lawns, we too grew respectfully silent. The lake near by was stiff and black, the waterfall frozen and still. We arranged ourselves shuffling around the big front door, then knocked and announced the Choir.

A maid bore the tidings of our arrival away into the echoing distances of the house, and while we waited we cleared our throats noisily. Then she came back, and the door was left ajar for us, and we were bidden to begin. We brought no music, the carols were in our heads. 'Let's give 'em "Wild Shepherds",' said Jack. We began in confusion, plunging into a wreckage of keys, of different words and tempo; but we gathered our strength; he who sang loudest took the rest of us with him, and the carol took shape if not sweetness.

This huge stone house, with its ivied walls, was always a mystery to us. What were those gables, those rooms and attics, those narrow windows veiled by the cedar trees? As we sang 'Wild Shepherds' we craned our necks, gaping into that lamplit hall which we had never entered; staring at the muskets and un-tenanted chairs, the great tapestries furred by dust—until suddenly, on the stairs, we saw the old Squire himself standing and listening with his head on one side.

He didn't move until we'd finished; then slowly he tottered towards us, dropped two coins in our box with a trembling hand, scratched his name in the book we carried, gave us each a long look with his moist blind eyes, then turned away in silence.

As though released from a spell, we took a few sedate steps, then broke into a run for the gate. We didn't stop till we were out of the grounds. Impatient, at last, to discover the extent of his bounty, we squatted by the cowsheds, held our lanterns over the book, and saw that he had written 'Two Shillings'. This was quite a good start. No one of any worth in the district would dare to give us less than the Squire.

So with money in the box, we pushed on up the valley, pouring scorn on each other's performance. Confident now, we began to consider our quality and whether one carol was not better suited to us than another. Horace, Walt said, shouldn't sing at all; his voice was beginning to break. Horace disputed this and there was a brief token battle—they fought as they walked, kicking up divots of snow, then they forgot it, and Horace still sang.

Steadily we worked through the length of the valley, going from house to house, visiting the lesser and the greater gentry— the farmers, the doctors, the merchants, the majors, and other exalted persons. It was freezing hard and blowing too; yet not for a moment did we feel the cold. The snow blew into our faces, into our eyes and mouths, soaked through our puttees, got into our boots, and dripped from our woollen caps. But we did not care. The collecting-box grew heavier, and the list of names in the book longer and more extravagant, each trying to outdo the other.

Mile after mile we went, fighting against the wind, falling into snowdrifts, and navigating by the lights of the houses. And yet we never saw our audience. We called at house after house; we sang in courtyards and porches, outside windows, or in the damp gloom of hallways; we heard voices from hidden rooms; we smelt rich clothes and strange hot food; we saw maids bearing in dishes or carrying away coffee-cups; we received nuts, cakes, figs, preserved ginger, dates, cough-drops, and money; but we never once saw our patrons. We sang as it were at the castle walls, and apart from the Squire, who had shown himself to prove that he was still alive, we never expected it otherwise.

As the night drew on there was trouble with Boney. 'Noël', for instance, had a rousing harmony which Boney persisted in singing, and singing flat. The others forbade him to sing it at all, and Boney said he would fight us. Picking himself up, he agreed we were right, then he disappeared altogether. He just turned away and walked into the snow and wouldn't answer when we called him back. Much later, as we reached a far point up the valley, somebody said 'Hark!' and we stopped to listen. Far away across the fields from the distant village came the sound of a frail voice singing, singing 'Noël', and singing it flat—it was Boney, branching out on his own.

We approached our last house high up on the hill, the place of Joseph the farmer. For him we had chosen a special carol, which was about the other Joseph, so that we always felt that singing it added a spicy cheek to the night. The last stretch of country to reach his farm was perhaps the most difficult of all. In these rough bare lanes, open to all winds, sheep were buried and wagons lost. Huddled together, we tramped in one another's footsteps, powdered snow blew into our screwed-up eyes, the candles burnt low, some blew out altogether, and we talked loudly above the gale.

Crossing, at last, the frozen mill-stream—whose wheel in summer still turned a barren mechanism—we climbed up to Joseph's farm. Sheltered by trees, warm on its bed of snow, it seemed always to be like this. As always it was late; as always this was our final call. The snow had a fine crust upon it, and the old trees sparkled like tinsel.

We grouped ourselves around the farmhouse porch. The sky cleared, and broad streams of stars ran down over the valley and away to Wales. On Slad's white slopes, seen through the black sticks of its woods, some red lamps still burned in the windows.

Everything was quiet; everywhere there was the faint crackling silence of the winter night. We started singing, and we were all moved by the words and the sudden trueness of our voices. Pure, very clear, and breathless, we sang:

> As Joseph was a walking
> He heard an angel sing;
> 'This night shall be the birth-time
> Of Christ the Heavenly King.
>
> He neither shall be bornèd
> In Housen nor in hall,
> Nor in a place of paradise
> But in an ox's stall . . .'

And two thousand Christmases became real to us then; the houses, the halls, the places of paradise had all been visited; the stars were bright to guide the Kings through the snow; and across the farmyard we could hear the beasts in their stalls. We were given roast apples and hot mince-pies, in our nostrils were spices like myrrh, and in our wooden box, as we headed back for the village, there were golden gifts for all.

Summer, June summer, with the green back on earth and the whole world unlocked and seething—like winter, it came suddenly and one knew it in bed, almost before waking up; with cuckoos and pigeons hollowing the woods since daylight and the chipping of tits in the pear-blossom.

On the bedroom ceiling, seen first through sleep, was a pool of expanding sunlight—the lake's reflection thrown up through the trees by the rapidly climbing sun. Still drowsy, I watched on the ceiling above me its glittering image reversed, saw every motion of its somnambulant waves and projections of the life upon it. Arrows ran across it from time to time, followed by the far call of a moorhen; I saw ripples of light around each root of the bulrushes, every detail of the lake seemed there. Then suddenly the whole picture would break into pieces, would be smashed like a molten mirror and run amok in tiny globules of gold, frantic and shivering; and I would hear the great slapping of wings on water, building up to a steady crescendo, while across the ceiling passed the shadows of swans taking off into the heavy morning. I would hear their cries pass over the house and watch the chaos of light above me, till it slowly settled and re-collected its stars and resumed the lake's still image.

Watching swans take off from my bedroom ceiling was a regular summer wakening. So I woke and looked out through the open window to a morning of cows and cockerels. The beech trees framing the lake and valley seemed to call for a Royal Hunt; but they served equally well for climbing into, and even in June you could still eat their leaves, a tight-folded salad of juices.

Outdoors, one scarcely knew what had happened or remembered any other time. There had never been rain, or frost, or cloud; it had always been like this. The heat from the ground climbed up one's legs and smote one under the chin. The garden, dizzy with scent and bees, burned all over with hot white flowers, each one so blinding an incandescence that it hurt the eyes to look at them . . .

We sat by the roadside and scooped the dust with our hands and made little piles in the gutters. Then we slid through the grass and lay on our backs and just stared at the empty sky. There was nothing to do. Nothing moved or happened, nothing happened at all except summer. Small heated winds blew over our faces, dandelion seeds floated by, burnt sap and roast nettles tingled our nostrils together with the dull rust smell of dry ground. The grass was June high and had come up with a rush, a massed entanglement of species, crested with flowers and spears of wild wheat, and coiled with clambering vetches, the whole of it humming with blundering bees and flickering with scarlet butter-flies. Chewing grass on our backs, the grass scaffolding the sky, the summer was all we heard; cuckoos crossed distances on chains of cries, flies buzzed and choked in the ears, and the saw-toothed chatter of mowing-machines drifted on waves of air from the fields . . .

Summer was also the time of these: of sudden plenty, of slow hours and actions, of diamond haze and dust on the eyes, of the valley in post-vernal slumber; of burying birds out of seething corruption; of Mother sleeping heavily at noon; of jazzing wasps and dragonflies, haystooks and thistle-seeds, snows of white butterflies, skylarks' eggs, bee-orchids and frantic ants; of wolf-cub parades, and boy-scout bugles; of sweat running down the legs; of boiling potatoes on bramble fires, of flames glass-blue in the sun; of lying naked in the hill-cold stream; begging pennies for bottles of pop; of girls' bare arms and unripe cherries, green apples and liquid walnuts; of fights and falls and new-scabbed knees, sobbing pursuits and flights; of picnics high up in the crumbling quarries, of butter running like oil, of sunstroke, fever, and cucumber peel stuck cool to one's burning brow. All this, and the feeling that it would never end, that such days had come for ever, with the pump drying up and the water-butt crawling, and the chalk ground hard as the moon. All sights twice-brilliant and smells twice as sharp, all game-days twice as long. Double charged as we were, like the meadow ants, with the frenzy of the sun, we used up the light to its last violet drop, and even then couldn't go to bed.

FRANK MANSELL

Stone Wall

For monument of native skill
In timeless texture living still,
For austere beauty, slowly grown,
Give me a wall of quarried stone.

A wall of Cotswold stone I mean,
With toppers set on edge and clean;
Not of the smooth cemented kind,
But stone, rough-hewn, with small to bind.

One of the walls that trophies bear
Of rusted scythe and worn-out share,
Of clay pipe stem and cattle bone,
Back to the times Napoleon.

A sturdy wall with middle filled,
The kind of wall they used to build
When horse and cart from quarry plied
The white lanes of the countryside.

A wall where truant tom-cats roam,
That hunting weasels know as home;
A wall where man may cool his head,
Or sleep beneath, or lie down dead.

Blaze on my shield, posterity,
A horse, a plough, a headland tree,
A furrow turned and, circling all,
A tidy stretch of dry stone wall!

From *Cotswold Ballads*

The mediaeval tower of Fowey parish church is the second highest in Cornwall, 119 feet. It looks down from the hill over the borough of Fowey, Quiller-Couch's Troy (which 'has a history and carries the marks of it') and the 'little grey sea town' of Kenneth Grahame's *The Wind in the Willows*.

This picture, entitled 'A Fish Sale on a Cornish Beach', was painted in 1885 by Stanhope Forbes, RA, who was said to have 'discovered' the fishing port of Newlyn in Mount's Bay, beyond Penzance. It became the home of a Cornish 'school' of painters. The picture here is in the City Art Gallery at Plymouth.

Not far from Jamaica Inn (on the Launceston–Bodmin road) we look across the spaces of Bodmin Moor of which E.C. Axford, its recent historian, has written: 'This small area which only measures about ten miles each way conveys a sense of loneliness and isolation quite out of proportion to its size.'

In the far centre of this picture of isolated Widecombe-in-the-Moor at the heart of winter there rises the great granite tower (120 feet) of the parish church. It was struck by lightning during an afternoon service on 21 October 1638: a terrifying storm during which four people in the congregation were killed and others (wrote John Prince in *The Worthies of Devon*) 'fell down in their seats, some upon their knees, others on their faces'.

During the mid-1830s J.M.W. Turner (1775–1851) painted this 'great vision of the guarded Mount'. St Michael's Mount, opposite Marazion, an island at high tide, is crowned romantically by a castle built upon the site of a Benedictine monastery. In the foreground, men are breaking up wrecked timber.

Carlyon Bay, on the south coast of Cornwall, is now the holiday outlet of the strange china-clay area, the White Country round St Austell. Close to Carlyon Bay is the little industrial port of Charlestown. Black Head is in the distance; the flowers in the foreground are montbretias.

Cornish tin mining was at its meridian during the nineteenth century. Now, when the prosperous days are over, many derelict mine buildings still remain, familiar silhouettes, as at Chapel Porth near St Agnes, on the north coast, where this photograph was taken.

Coverack, by its wide cove, not the usual cleft, is a serene fishing village in what is still one of the lesser-known parts of Cornwall. The east coast of the Lizard peninsula is the setting of Quiller-Couch's story, 'The Roll-Call of the Reef'.

Sean O'Casey, the Irish dramatist, who lived for seventeen years at Totnes—seen here from the Castle ramparts—said: 'Gentleness is the first quality to give to it; gentleness in its buildings, and in the coming and going of its people; and in the slow winding, winding of the River Dart from the moor to the sea.'

EVELYN WAUGH

Boot Magna

Evelyn Waugh's novel *Scoop* (1938) is the tale of William Boot, of Boot Magna Hall, Somerset. Mildest of writers on natural history ('Feather-footed through the plashy fens passes the questing vole'), he finds himself, by editorial error, covering the civil war in the African Republic of Ishmaelia for the *Daily Beast*. When the campaign is over and Boot, more surprised than anyone, has 'scooped' all rivals, there are dire complications at the office of the *Beast*. Mr Salter, the foreign editor, has to go hurriedly to Boot Magna to explain.

. . . William found Mr Salter's telegram waiting for him on the breakfast table.

His mother, Priscilla, and his three uncles sat round the table. They had finished eating and were sitting there, as they often sat for an hour or so, doing nothing at all. Priscilla alone was occupied, killing wasps in the honey on her plate.

'There's a telegram for you,' said his mother. 'We were wondering whether we ought to open it or send it up to you.'

It said: MUST SEE YOU IMMEDIATELY URGENT BUSINESS ARRIVING BOOT MAGNA HALT TOMORROW AFTERNOON 6.10 SALTER.

The message was passed from hand to hand around the table.

Mrs Boot said, 'Who is Mr Salter, and what urgent business can he possibly have here?'

Uncle Roderick said, 'He can't stay the night. Nowhere for him to sleep.'

Uncle Bernard said, 'You must telegraph and put him off.'

Uncle Theodore said, 'I knew a chap called Salter once, but I don't suppose it's the same one.'

Priscilla said, 'I believe he means to come today. It's dated yesterday.'

'He's the foreign editor of the *Beast*,' William explained. 'The one I told you about who sent me abroad.'

'He must be a very pushful fellow, inviting himself here like this. Anyway, as Roderick says, we've no room for him.'

'We could send Priscilla to the Caldicotes for the night.'

'I like that,' said Priscilla, adding illogically, 'Why don't you send William, it's his friend.'

'Yes,' said Mrs Boot. 'Priscilla could go to the Caldicotes.'

'I'm cubbing tomorrow,' said Priscilla, 'right in the other direction. You can't expect Lady Caldicote to send me thirty miles at eight in the morning.'

For over an hour the details of Priscilla's hunt occupied the dining-room. Could she send her horse overnight to a farm near the meet; could she leave the Caldicotes at dawn, pick up her horse at Boot Magna, and ride on; could she borrow Major Watkins's trailer and take her horse to the Caldicotes for the night, then as far as Major Watkins's in the morning and ride on from there; if she got the family car from Aunt Agnes and Major Watkins's trailer, would Lady Caldicote lend her a car to take it to Major Watkins's; would Aunt Anne allow the car to stay the night; would she discover it was taken without her permission? They discussed the question exhaustively, from every angle; Troutbeck twice glowered at them from the door and finally began to clear the table; Mr Salter and the object of his visit were not mentioned.

That evening, some time after the advertised hour, Mr Salter alighted at Boot Magna Halt. An hour earlier, at Taunton, he had left the express and changed into a train such as he did not know existed outside the imagination of his Balkan correspondents; a single tram-like, one-class coach, which had pottered in a desultory fashion through a system of narrow, under-populated valleys. It had stopped eight times, and at every station there had been a bustle of passengers succeeded by a long, silent pause, before it started again; men had entered who, instead of slinking and shuffling and wriggling themselves into corners and decently screening themselves behind newspapers, as civilised people should when they travelled by train, had sat down squarely quite close to Mr Salter, rested their hands on their knees, stared at him fixedly and uncritically, and suddenly addressed him on the subject of the weather in barely intelligible accents; there had been very old, unhygienic men and women, such as you never saw in the Underground, who ought long ago to have been put away in some public institution; there had been women carrying a multitude of atrocious little baskets and parcels which they piled on the seats; one of them had put a hamper containing a live turkey under Mr Salter's feet. It had been a horrible journey.

At last, with relief, Mr Salter alighted. He lifted his suitcase from among the sinister bundles on the rack and carried it to the centre of the platform. There was no one else for Boot Magna. Mr Salter had hoped to find William waiting to meet him, but the little station was empty except for a single porter who was leaning against the cab of the engine engaged in a kind of mute, telepathic converse with the driver, and a cretinous native youth who stood on the further side of the paling, leant against it, and picked at the dry paint-bubbles with a toe-like thumb nail. When Mr Salter looked at him, he glanced away and grinned wickedly at his boots.

The train observed its customary two minutes' silence and then steamed slowly away. The porter shuffled across the line and disappeared into a hut labelled 'Lamps'. Mr Salter turned towards the palings; the youth was still leaning there, gazing; his eyes dropped; he grinned. Three times, shuttlecock fashion, they alternately glanced up and down till Mr Salter, with urban impatience, tired of the flirtation and spoke up.

'I say.'

'Ur.'

'Do you happen to know whether Mr Boot has sent a car for me?'

'Ur.'

'He has?'

'Noa. She've a taken of the harse.'

'I am afraid you misunderstand me.' Mr Salter's voice sounded curiously flutey and querulous in contrast to the deep tones of the moron. 'I'm coming to visit Mr Boot. I wondered if he had sent a motor-car for me.'

'He've a sent me.'

'With the car?'

'Noa. Motor-car's over to Lady Caldicote's taking of the harse. The bay,' he explained, since Mr Salter seemed not to be satisfied with this answer. 'Had to be the bay for because the mare's sick . . . The old bay's not up yet,' he added as though to make everything perfectly clear.

'Well, how am I to get to the house?'

'Why, along of me and Bert Tyler.'

'Has this Mr Tyler got a car, then?'

'Noa. I tell e car's over to Lady Caldicote's along of Miss Priscilla and the bay . . . Had to be the bay,' he persisted, 'because the mare's sick.'

'Yes, yes, I quite appreciate that.'

'And the old bay's still swole up with grass. So you'm to ride along of we.'

'Ride?' A hideous vision rose before Mr Salter.

'Ur. Along of me and Bert Tyler and the slag.'

'Slag?'

'Ur. Mr Roderick's getting in the slag now for to slag Westerheys. Takes a tidy bit.'

Mr Salter was suffused with relief. 'You mean that you have some kind of vehicle outside full of slag?'

'Ur. Cheaper now than what it will be when Mr Roderick wants it.'

Mr Salter descended the steps into the yard where, out of sight from the platform, an open lorry was standing; an old man next to the driving seat touched his cap; the truck was loaded high with sacks; bonnet and back bore battered learner plates. The youth took Mr Salter's suitcase and heaved it up among the slag. 'You'm to ride behind,' he said.

'If it's all the same to you,' said Mr Salter rather sharply, 'I should prefer to sit in front.'

'It's all the same to me, but I dursn't let you. The police would have I.'

'Good gracious, why?'

'Bert Tyler have to ride along of me, for because of the testers.'

'Testers?'

'Ur. Police don't allow for me to drive except along of Bert Tyler. Bert Tyler he've a had a licence twenty year. There wasn't no testers for Bert Tyler. But police they took and tested I over to Taunton.'

'And you failed?'

A great grin spread over the young man's face. 'I busted tester's leg for he,' he said proudly. 'Ran he bang into the wall, going a fair lick.'

'Oh, dear. Wouldn't it be better for your friend Tyler to drive us?'

'Noa. He can't see for to drive, Bert Tyler can't. Don't e be afeared. I can *see* all right. It be the corners do for I.'

'And are there many corners between here and the house?'

'Tidy few.'

Mr Salter, who had had his foot on the hub of the wheel preparatory to mounting, now drew back. His nerve, never strong, had been severely tried that afternoon; now it failed him.

'I'll walk,' he said. 'How far is it?'

'Well, it's all according as you know the way. We do call it three mile over the fields. It's a tidy step by the road.'

'Perhaps you'll be good enough to show me the field path?'

'Tain't exactly what you would call a path. 'E just keeps straight.'

'Well, I daresay I shall find it. If . . . if by any chance you get to the house before me, will you tell Mr Boot that I wanted a little exercise after the journey?'

The learner-driver looked at Mr Salter with undisguised contempt. 'I'll tell e as you was afeared to ride along of me and Bert Tyler,' he said.

Mr Salter stepped back into the station porch to avoid the dust as the lorry drove away. It was as well that he did so, for, as he mounted the incline, the driver mistakenly changed into reverse and the machine charged precipitately back in its tracks, and came noisily to rest against the wall where Mr Salter had been standing. The second attempt was more successful and it reached the lane with no worse damage than a mudguard crushed against the near gatepost.

Then with rapid, uncertain steps Mr Salter set out on his walk to the house.

It was eight o'clock when Mr Salter arrived at the front door. He had covered a good six miles tacking from field to field under the setting sun; he had scrambled through fences and ditches; in one enormous pasture a herd of cattle had closed silently in on him and followed at his heels—the nearest not a yard away—with lowered heads and heavy breath; Mr Salter had broken into a run and they had trotted after him; when he gained the stile and turned to face them, they began gently grazing in his tracks; dogs had flown at him in three farmyards where he had stopped to ask the way, and to be misdirected; at last, when he felt he could go no further but must lie down and perish from exposure under the open sky, he had stumbled through an overgrown stile to find himself in the main road with the lodge gates straight ahead; the last mile up the drive had been the bitterest of all.

And now he stood under the porch, sweating, blistered, nettle-stung, breathless, parched, dizzy, dead-beat and dishevelled, with his bowler hat in one hand and umbrella in the other, leaning against a stucco pillar waiting for someone to open the door. Nobody came. He pulled again at the bell; there was no answering ring, no echo in the hall beyond. No sound broke the peace of the evening save, in the elms that stood cumbrously on every side, the crying of the rooks, and, not unlike it but nearer at hand, directly it seemed over Mr Salter's head, a strong baritone decanting irregular snatches of sacred music.

'In Thy courts no more are needed, sun by day nor moon by night,' sang Uncle Theodore blithely, stepping into his evening trousers; he remembered it as a treble solo rising to the dim vaults of the school chapel, touching the toughest adolescent hearts; he remembered it imperfectly but with deep emotion.

Mr Salter listened, unmoved. In despair he began to pound the front door with his umbrella. The singing ceased and the voice in fruity, more prosaic tones demanded, 'What, ho, without there?'

Mr Salter hobbled down the steps, clear of the porch, and saw framed in the ivy of a first-floor window, a ruddy, Hanoverian face and plump, bare torso. 'Good evening,' he said politely.

'Good-evening.' Uncle Theodore leaned out as far as he safely could and stared at Mr Salter through a monocle. 'From where you are standing,' he said, 'you might easily take me to be totally undraped. Let me hasten to assure you that such is not the case.

Seemly black shrouds me from the waist down. No doubt you
are the friend my nephew William is expecting?'

'Yes . . . I've been ringing the bell.'

'It sounded to me,' said Uncle Theodore severely, 'as though
you were hammering the door with a stick.'

'Yes, I was. You see . . .'

'You'll be late for dinner, you know, if you stand out there
kicking up a rumpus. And so shall I if I stay talking to you. We
will meet again shortly in more conventional circumstances. For
the moment—*a rivederci.*'

The head withdrew and once more the melody rose into the
twilight, mounted to the encircling tree-tops and joined the
chorus of the homing rooks.

Mr Salter tried the handle of the door. It opened easily. Never
in his life had he made his own way into anyone else's house.
Now he did so and found himself in a lobby cluttered with
implements of sport, overcoats, rugs, a bicycle or two and a
stuffed bear. Beyond it, glass doors led him into the hall. He was
dimly aware of a shadowy double staircase which rose and spread
before him, of a large, carpetless chequer of black and white
marble pavings, of islands of furniture and some potted palms.
Quite near the glass doors stood a little arm-chair where no one
ever sat; there Mr Salter sank and there he was found twenty
minutes later by William's mother when she came down to dinner.
His last action before he lapsed into a coma had been to remove
his shoes.

JANE AUSTEN

Conversation at Bath

Early in Jane Austen's *Northanger Abbey* (published posthumously in 1818) Catherine Morland and Isabella Thorpe are talking in the Pump Room at Bath. Their subject is the fashionable 'tale of terror' of which Mrs Ann Radcliffe, who wrote the wildly Gothic *Mysteries of Udolpho* was one of the most admired inventors. We remember her unexpected appearance in a line and a half from Byron's *Childe Harold*, on the city of Venice: 'And Otway, Radcliffe, Schiller, Shakespeare's art,/Had stamp'd her image in me.'

The following conversation, which took place between the two friends in the Pump Room one morning, after an acquaintance of eight or nine days, is given as a specimen of their very warm attachment, and of the delicacy, discretion, originality of thought, and literary taste which marked the reasonableness of that attachment.

They met by appointment; and as Isabella had arrived nearly five minutes before her friend, her first address naturally was— 'My dearest creature, what can have made you so late? I have been waiting for you at least this age!'

'Have you indeed? I am very sorry for it, but really I thought I was in very good time. It is but just one. I hope you have not been here long?'

'Oh! these ten ages, at least. I am sure I have been here this half-hour. But now, let us go and sit down at the other end of the room, and enjoy ourselves. I have a hundred things to say to you. In the first place, I was so afraid it would rain this morning, just as I wanted to set off; it looked very showery, and that would have thrown me into agonies. Do you know, I saw the prettiest hat you can imagine in a shop window in Milsom Street just now— very like yours, only with coquelicot ribands instead of green; I quite longed for it. But, my dearest Catherine, what have you been doing with yourself all this morning? Have you gone on with *Udolpho?*'

'Yes, I have been reading it ever since I woke; and I am got to the black veil.'

'Are you indeed? How delightful! Oh, I would not tell you what is behind the black veil for the world! Are not you wild to know?'

'Oh! yes, quite; what can it be? But do not tell me. I would not be told upon any account. I know it must be a skeleton; I am sure it is Laurentina's skeleton. Oh, I am delighted with the book! I should like to spend my whole life in reading it, I assure you; if it had not been to meet you, I would not have come away from it for all the world.'

'Dear creature, how much I am obliged to you! and when you have finished *Udolpho,* we will read the Italian together; and I have made out a list of ten or twelve more of the same kind for you.'

'Have you indeed? How glad I am! What are they all?'

'I will read you their names directly. Here they are, in my pocket-book: *Castle of Wolfenbach, Clermont, Mysterious Warnings, Necromancer of the Black Forest, Midnight Bell, Orphan of the Rhine,* and *Horrid Mysteries.* Those will last us some time.'

'Yes, pretty well; but are they all horrid? are you sure they are all horrid?'

'Yes, quite sure; for a particular friend of mine, a Miss Andrews, a sweet girl, one of the sweetest creatures in the world, has read every one of them. I wish you knew Miss Andrews; you would be delighted with her. She is netting herself the sweetest cloak you can conceive. I think her as beautiful as an angel, and I am so vexed with the men for not admiring her. I scold them all amazingly about it.'

'Scold them! Do you scold them for not admiring her?'

'Yes, that I do. There is nothing I would not do for those who are really my friends. I have no notion of loving people by halves; it is not my nature. My attachments are always excessively strong. I told Captain Hunt at one of our assemblies this winter that if he was to tease me all night I would not dance with him unless he would allow Miss Andrews to be as beautiful as an angel. The men think us incapable of real friendship, you know; and I am determined to show them the difference. Now, if I were to hear anybody speak slightingly of you, I should fire up in a moment; but that is not at all likely, for *you* are just the kind of girl to be a great favourite with the men.'

'Oh dear!' cried Catherine, colouring; 'how can you say so?'

'I know you very well: you have so much animation, which is exactly what Miss Andrews wants; for I must confess there is something amazingly insipid about her. Oh! I must tell you that, just after we parted yesterday, I saw a young man looking at you so earnestly, I am sure he is in love with you.' Catherine coloured, and disclaimed again. Isabella laughed. 'It is very true, upon my honour; but I see how it is: you are indifferent to everybody's admiration, except that of one gentleman, who shall be nameless. Nay, I cannot blame you' (speaking more seriously); 'your feelings are easily understood. Where the heart is really attached, I know very well how little one can be pleased with the attention of anybody else. Everything is so insipid, so uninteresting, that does not relate to the beloved object! I can perfectly comprehend your feelings.'

'But you should not persuade me that I think so very much about Mr Tilney, for perhaps I may never see him again.'

'Not see him again! My dearest creature, do not talk of it. I am sure you would be miserable if you thought so.'

'No, indeed; I should not. I do not pretend to say that I was not very much pleased with him; but while I have *Udolpho* to read, I feel as if nobody could make me miserable. Oh, the dreadful black veil! My dear Isabella, I am sure there must be Laurentina's skeleton behind it.'

'It is so odd to me that you should never have read *Udolpho* before; but I suppose Mrs Morland objects to novels.'

'No, she does not. She very often reads *Sir Charles Grandison* herself; but new books do not fall in our way.'

'*Sir Charles Grandison!* That is an amazing horrid book, is it not? I remember Miss Andrews could not get through the first volume.'

'It is not like *Udolpho* at all; but yet I think it is very entertaining.'

'Do you indeed? You surprise me. I thought it had not been readable. But, my dearest Catherine, have you settled what to wear on your head tonight? I am determined, at all events, to be dressed exactly like you. The men take notice of *that* sometimes, you know.'

'But it does not signify if they do,' said Catherine very innocently.

'Signify! O heavens! I make it a rule never to mind what they say. They are very often amazingly impertinent, if you do not treat them with spirit, and make them keep their distance.'

'Are they? Well, I never observed *that*. They always behave very well to me.'

'Oh! they give themselves such airs. They are the most con-ceited creatures in the world, and think themselves of so much importance! By-the-bye, though I have thought of it a hundred times, I have always forgot to ask you what is your favourite complexion in a man. Do you like them best dark or fair?'

'I hardly know. I never much thought about it. Something between both, I think: brown—not fair, and not very dark.'

'Very well, Catherine. That is exactly he. I have not forgot your description of Mr Tilney: "a brown skin, with dark eyes, and rather dark hair." Well, my taste is different. I prefer light eyes; and as to complexion—do you know—I like a sallow better than any other. You must not betray me, if you should ever meet with one of your acquaintance answering that description.'

'Betray you! What do you mean?'

'Nay, do not distress me. I believe I have said too much. Let us drop the subject.'

Catherine, in some amazement, complied; and after remaining a few moments silent, was on the point of reverting to what interested her at that time rather more than anything else in the world—Laurentina's skeleton—when her friend prevented her by saying, 'For Heaven's sake, let us move away from this end of the room. Do you know, there are two odious young men who have been staring at me this half-hour. They really put me quite out of countenance. Let us go and look at the arrivals. They will hardly follow us there.'

Away they walked to the book; and while Isabella examined the names, it was Catherine's employment to watch the proceedings of these alarming young men.

'They are not coming this way, are they? I hope they are not so impertinent as to follow us. Pray let me know if they are coming. I am determined I will not look up.'

In a few moments Catherine, with unaffected pleasure, assured her that she need not be longer uneasy, as the gentlemen had just left the Pump Room.

'And which way are they gone?' said Isabella, turning hastily round. 'One was a very good-looking young man.'

'They went towards the churchyard.'

'Well, I am amazingly glad I have got rid of them! And now, what say you to going to Edgar's Buildings with me, and looking at my new hat? You said you should like to see it.'

Catherine readily agreed. 'Only,' she added, 'perhaps we may overtake the two young men.'

'Oh! never mind that. If we make haste, we shall pass by them presently, and I am dying to show you my hat.'

'But if we only wait a few minutes, there will be no danger of our seeing them at all.'

'I shall not pay them any such compliment, I assure you. I have no notion of treating men with such respect. *That* is the way to spoil them.'

Catherine had nothing to oppose against such reasoning; and therefore, to show the independence of Miss Thorpe, and her resolution of humbling the sex, they set off immediately as fast as they could walk, in pursuit of the two young men.

DAPHNE DU MAURIER

Bodmin Moor

Dame Daphne du Maurier (Lady Browning), from whose study of *Vanishing Cornwall* (1967) we take this extract, is a daughter of the famous actor-manager, Sir Gerald du Maurier. She has lived for many years in Cornwall, the scene of some of her most re-nowned novels, *Jamaica Inn* (1936), *Rebecca* (1938), and *Frenchman's Creek* (1941) among them.

The whole of Cornwall's backbone, running from the source of Tamar in Stratton Hundred in the north to the descending land in the south-west where the rising Hayle divides Kirrier from Penwith, was once moor or downland, and the motorist who takes the main road today, remembering that he follows the route of pack-horse, mule and ox in centuries gone by, will notice that he is always on high ground. There are wooded valleys between the folds of hills; towns and villages are built on either side of his approach, but if the latter were swept away the land beneath them would be moorland scrub.

The backbone is, in fact, a high plateau, descending slowly as Cornwall narrows, only to rise and broaden out with Goonhilly Downs behind the Lizard peninsula, and again to the highlands of West Penwith and the Land's End claw.

The greatest and wildest stretch of moorland is the land mass south of Launceston, north of Bodmin, reaching east as far as Liskeard and west beyond Camelford almost to Tintagel and the coast. The main road cuts across the centre from Five Lanes, and in summer a stream of cars and coaches passes along it with holiday-makers coastward bound, but in winter the road is almost as free from traffic as it was in earlier days. Rough tracks lead to isolated farms whose inhabitants once hardly ventured forth except to market, owners of sheep and cattle who lived on their own produce and cut moorland turf for fuel. The wanderer who is fond of solitude can wander anywhere on either side of the main road and lose himself forthwith, turning, after he has walked barely half a mile in open country, to see no sign of human habitation, nothing but bare brown moor as far as the eye can reach, rising in the distance to frowning tors and craggy rocks that might give shelter if a rain-shower came, but little comfort from the wind which seeks out clefts and crannies even if the day is still.

Brown Willy, 1,375 feet, and Rough Tor, its companion near to Camelford, are the highest hills, often climbed by straggling parties in a dry season, the views stupendous when the weather is clear, stretching to the coasts on either side and away down the peninsula past the china-clay pyramids almost as far as West Penwith. The river Fowey rises beneath Brown Willy, and originally the whole district was known as Fawey moor. The ground here is soggy, treacherous, betraying its presence by a darker green and tufts of grass, sometimes with reedy stems, which to the ignorant might seem as firm as the coarser tussocks of the higher ground near by, until weight put upon them makes them sag, tremble, and sink to oozing water. Deception is all around, for the turf one has just travelled no longer appears safe but trembles too, and panic sets in with each faltering step. The secret is never to descend, if possible, to what seems smooth and easy pasture lying low, for here are the intersecting streams, the bogs, marshes, traps not only for the walker but for straying sheep and cattle that in a wet winter are imprisoned, lost, their carcasses fed upon by the more wily fox or plucked from above by hawk and buzzard until nothing remains but bones and skull bleached white.

The moorland east of the main road, above the Fowey stream and the Withey Brook, is even more hazardous, for the walker sets off in good heart on high and firm land, believing he has only to traverse the plateau to find himself, after five miles or so, on the wooded slopes of Trebartha and North Hill village. Instead, the woods remain a mirage only. Crags more menacing and bleak than Brown Willy and Rough Tor loom before him, barring progress, and instinct, almost invariably wrong on these occasions, directs him to walk to the right, where the ground descends, and stops him in mid-track again, for here is another stream, another marsh, and to pursue this track petering into bog can only lead to disaster. I know, for I have tried it.

Foolheartedly, long ago, on a November afternoon, a friend and I . . . departed on horseback from Jamaica Inn with the happy intention of calling on an elderly lady living at Trebartha Hall near North Hill. Surely, we told ourselves, it would be no more than forty minutes' ride at most; and if we stayed to tea then we must make up our minds to skirt the moor on our homeward track, and jog back to Jamaica Inn by road. Irresponsible, we trotted off across the moor no later than two o'clock, only to find after an hour or more that we were little nearer to our destination, that tors and boulders inaccessible on horseback, even perhaps on foot, barred our passage. The track leading us on descended to a slippery path that disappeared, while beneath us a battered gate swinging by the hinges, gave access to a swollen stream. The day, comparatively fine until that moment, darkened, and a black cloud, trailing ribbons, hovered above our heads and burst.

In a moment all was desolation. The ominous stream rushed by with greater swiftness, turning to a torrent. Forcing the horses up a steep incline, to put distance between ourselves and the running water, our heads bent low to our saddles, we plunged onward, seeking escape. A deserted cottage, humped beneath the hill, seemed our only hope—at least it would be temporary refuge until the cloudburst ceased. We rode towards it, dismounted, and led our horses to the rear. The cottage was not only empty but part fallen, with rain driving through the empty windows, and what roof there had been was repaired with corrugated tin, so that the cascading rain sounded like hailstones on its surface. We leant against the fungoid walls and brooded, Trebartha Hall a hundred miles away, Jamaica Inn an equal distance, and all the while the rain fell upon the corrugated roof to echo in a splashing water-butt near by. I had never known greater despondency.

It rained for a full hour, then turned to drizzle and dank fog, by which time our world was murky and we had lost all sense of compass points. Emerging from the ruins my companion, a better horsewoman than I and owner of both our steeds, looked about her and observed, 'There's nothing for it but to get into the saddle, leave our reins loose on their necks, and let them lead us home.'

I was not impressed by her suggestion, for where was home to the horses—thirty miles or more to Fowey, or back across the moors to Jamaica Inn? We mounted once more, darkness and silence all about us, save for that dreary patter on the cottage roof, and somewhere to our right the hissing stream.

The horses, sure-footed even amongst dead heather and loose stones, plodded forward without hesitation, and there was some relief at least to be away from the abandoned cottage and in the open, however desolate, for there had been no warmth within its walls, no memories of hearths glowing with turf fire kindled by its owners in the past. Surely whoever lived there before he let it fall to ruins had been sullen and morose, plagued by the Withey Brook that ran somewhere below his door, and in despair went out one night and drowned himself. I suggested this to my fellow-traveller, who was not amused, especially as the horses seemed attracted to the river sound. Gaining higher ground we found ourselves facing a new hazard in the form of what appeared to be a disused railway track, upon which our mounts slithered and stumbled. A railroad in mid-moor. It could not be. Unless we had both gone mad and this was fantasy.

'A line for trolleys,' said my companion, 'leading to a stone-quarry. If the horses take us there they'll break their legs. Better dismount.' Bogs, quarries, brooks, boulders, hell on every side, we led the horses from the slippery track and then got up on our saddles once again. I remembered an illustration from a book read long ago in childhood, *Sintram, and His Companions*, where a dispirited knight had travelled such a journey with the devil in disguise, who called himself The Little Master. It showed a terrified steed rearing near a precipice. This was to be our fate, and The Little Master would come and claim us.

The horses, bolder now that they were free of the trolley-lines, headed steadily forward, straight across the moor, possibly in the direction of those menacing crags that we had seen in early afternoon, pointing dark fingers to the sky, which, we knew very well, lay contrary to any path for home.

It was seven, it was nine, it was midnight—too dark to see our watches, and fumbling fingers could not strike damp matches. On, forever on, nothing on all sides but waste and moor.

Suddenly my companion cried, 'They've done it . . . they've done it . . . Isn't that the road?'

Peering into the darkness ahead, I saw a break in the rising ground, and a new flatness, and there, not a hundred yards distant, the blessed streaky wetness of the Launceston-Bodmin road, and surprisingly, unbelievably, the gaunt chimneys of Jamaica Inn itself.

'I told you so,' called the expert, 'horses always know the way. They travel by instinct. See, the people from the Inn have come to look for us', and sure enough there were figures with tossing lanterns wandering to and fro upon the road, and welcoming lamplight shone from the slated porch. In an instant fear was forgotten, danger had never been. It was just eight o'clock, the landlord and his wife had only then begun to think of us, and here was the turf fire for which we had longed, brown and smoky sweet, a supper of eggs and bacon ready to be served with a pot of scalding tea.

Today all is changed, and, as the poet Yeats once said, 'changed utterly'. Motor-coaches, cars, electric light, a bar, dinner of river-trout, baths for the travel-stained instead of a cream-jug of hot water. As a motorist I pass by with some embarrassment, feeling myself to blame, for out of that November evening long ago came a novel which proved popular, passing, as fiction does, into the folk-lore of the district. As the author I am flattered, but as a one-time wanderer dismayed.

Trebartha Hall, where we had hoped to call that afternoon, was pulled down some years ago, while the craggy hills that seemed to bar our progress, Trewortha Tor, Hawk's Tor, Kilmar Tor, frown down upon the landscape with less malevolence when approached from the east, and are easily reached by a steep car-climb from North Hill village, and then a brief trek on foot. The approach from the front that we tried still appears hazardous, but hardly stuff for nightmare, unless we had indeed ventured to traverse the dreaded Withey Brook and the formidable marsh to which it leads. As for the trolley-track, diligent search has revealed no trace of it— the quarries were much further south, and out of our range. Whether we were nearer to Jamaica Inn than we imagined, or further away, is something I shall never discover; all I know is that beyond Withey Brook, between the largest tors, lies the romantic-sounding Twelve Men's Moor, teeming with granite boulders and broken stones, plashed about with seeping bogs. If this was where we rode in darkness, my salutation is overdue to the dozen men who in 1284 held it from Henry, Prior of Launceston. The land was granted to them at a rate of four silver shillings a year, to be paid at Michaelmas, in return for homage and service, and the twelve men had their farms spaced out with the right of pasture over it.

Thomas and David of Kelnystok, William Foth, Robert Faber, Jordan Cada, Robert Broda, Walter la Lak, Robert Le Legha, Roger Boglawoda, John Can, William of Trewortha, Nicholas Cada—here are names for the etymologist; perhaps Walter la Lak had his farm bodering a stream, and beneath that now abandoned cottage with the corrugated roof would be thirteenth-century foundations. Life was never easy for the moorland farmer, though wool in earlier days might have fetched a price, had he stock enough to make it worth his while. But summer as well as winter would take toll of his beasts, and he needed greater courage and staying power than the farmer in the valley.

When the Twelve Men lived upon the moor there was, a few miles to the west of them, a chapel known in Edward I's day as the Capella de Temple. This was the property of the Knights Templars of Jerusalem, who by nature of their fraternity assisted all pilgrims and strangers who wished to visit the Sepulchre in the Holy Land. The chapel was built for the repose of such pilgrims, for worship and for contemplation, and was exempt from the Bishop's jurisdiction. The vicar or curate at Temple could marry without banns or licence anyone who applied to him, and, since the chapel was near to the only road across the moors between Launceston and Bodmin, this made it handy for those who wished to take advantage of its privileges. 'Lying in a wild wastrell, exempted from the Bishop's Jurisdiction, many a bad marriage bargain is there yearly slubbered up; and grass widows with their fatlings put to lie and nurse here,' wrote the chronicler Tonkin.

Between Temple and Twelve Men's Moor the wayfarer in the past (or the motorist today, for a road skirts close to it) found himself surprised by an inland lake, a mile in circumference, lying in a flat hollow between the hills. This is Dozmare Pool, a sheet of water that people in old days believed bottomless; and because of it legend grew that this was where Bedivere threw the sword Excalibur, seized in mid-lake by a thrice-waving hand which fastened upon the hilt and then withdrew to unplumbed depths. Pagan myth, older than the Arthur story, said that a giant chieftain who bade his daughters slay their husbands on their marriage-night had his hunting-grounds near by, but the gods, displeased with his command, doomed him for evermore to empty the waters of the pool with a limpet-shell. In time tradition placed this punishment upon a real personage, John Tregeagle, steward to Lord Robartes of Lanhydrock in the seventeenth century, hated by all the tenants, and so the stories spread and grew, became confused, turning the pool for all time to a place of uneasy memories.

Dozmare has many moods. It is still and limpid on a summer's day, tempting to the paddler, but once a whisper of a breeze ripples the surface the colour changes to a slaty grey, ominous and drear, and little wavelets splash the shore, pebbled with brown stones and peaty mud. Then we forget that it is only five feet deep, and look for the rising hand to break the surface, reaching for Excalibur, or listen for the thin note of a demon's hunting-horn, calling hounds to the chase, pursuing the chieftain-giant, so the legend runs, some sixteen miles westward across the moors to Roche.

CHARLES CAUSLEY

On
Launceston Castle

Charles Causley, born in Launceston where he still lives (and was
for many years a schoolmaster), is a major English poet, author of
many books, and an Hon D Lit of Exeter University. In 1967 he
was awarded the Queen's Gold Medal for Poetry. He has written
this poem especially for *The West Country Book*.

Winded, on this blue stack
Of downward-drifting stone,
The unwashed sky a low-
Slung blanket thick with rain,
I search the cold, unclear
Vernacular of clay,
Water and woods and rock:
The primer of my day.

Westward, a cardiograph
Of granite, Bodmin Moor;
Its sharp, uncertain stream
Knifing the valley floor.
Ring-dove and jackdaw rise
Over the blackboys' bell;
Circle, in jostling air,
The town's stopped carousel.

The quarry's old wound, plugged
With brambles is long-dry.
Dark bands of ivy scale
The torn school; lichens try
The building on for size.
Beyond the weir, a rout
Of barrack-tinted homes
Cancels a meadow out.

Down from the ribbed hill-crest
Combers of grasses ride.
Poppy, valerian
Bleed by the lean lake-side.
Allotments, in a slum
Of weeds and willows, keep
Scrupulous house. I note
A pinch of cows, of sheep.

Vociferous with paint,
A flock of ploughs supplies
Unlocal colour, where
The shut pond slowly dies.
Below the morning's saw-
Edged scope of birches, pines,
The hour is alchemised.
The hurt sun mends. It shines.

This was my summer stage:
Childhood and youth the play,
Its text a fable told
When time was far away.
But once I was too young
And still am too unsure
To cast a meaning from
The town's hard metaphor.

I cannot read between
The lines of leaf and stone,
For these are other eyes
And the swift light has gone.
By my birth-place the stream
Rubs a wet flank, breaks free
From the moored wall; escapes,
Unwavering, to sea.

CHRISTOPHER FRY

Looking Westward

It has been said of Christopher Fry, one of the few very fine English verse dramatists of the century, that he again showed dramatic poetry how to dance: see, for example, *The Lady's Not For Burning* (1948) and *Venus Observed* (1950). But he has written in many moods (*A Sleep of Prisoners*, 1950; *Curtmantle*, 1962). His book *Can You Find Me: A Family History*, appeared in 1977. For many years President of the West Country Writers' Association, he offers these 'notes claiming West-Countryhood'.

If, as he did, my father's grandfather came from Salcombe where the family had been bargemen from the eighteenth century or earlier; and if, as he did, my mother's grandfather came from Axbridge, where, or thereabouts, the family had lived from the fifteenth century, if not longer, am I not a West Countryman, in spite of other injections of blood from Surrey and Kent? And doesn't my birth in Bristol go some way to settling the matter?

It is true that from the age of three I was deprived of my birthright, but my father, though born in Kent, was buried in Ilfracombe, and his Kentish brother, my Uncle Bert, made a move towards redemption by becoming in later life the Mayor of Penryn. When I was eleven or twelve we spent a holiday week with him and Aunt Nell. It was the week when the town danced the Floral Dance up and down the street and in and out of the houses. Nothing like that ever happened in Gladstone Street, Bedford, where we came from. I gorged myself on saffron cakes and Cornish pasties.

There are other fragments of western memory. The summer of 1929 when the headmaster of the prep school I was teaching at, his wife and children, his wife's niece Mary Taylor, Michael Tippett, who taught French at the school, and I, all met together in Cornwall. Mary was staying with a bachelor uncle in a cottage made out of an old chapel. He wore a red beard and even redder socks. I stayed with them for two or three nights, sleeping on a truckle bed just inside the front door. I awoke to the postman dropping the morning letters on to my chest. Mary and I took a seven-mile walk to Polperro, getting back in time to go to the fair at Fowey for the second evening in succession. 'The Quiller-Couches were there,' I wrote in a letter to my mother, 'Q, his wife and a daughter called Foy, and Angela du Maurier. Mary met her sailor and he took her on the swings, so I found my Spanish girl and took *her* (keeping a firm eye on Mary and the sailor) on the roundabouts.' And I remember walking with Michael Tippett on a wide deserted beach—'a sea of glass like unto crystal' and wet dazzling sands; there was nothing of the world but space and light. I felt myself close to levitation. Tippett said he always knew when the train he was travelling in crossed the border from Devon into Cornwall, even with his eyes shut; the magic of the duchy penetrated his eyelids.

In the summer of 1932 Robert Gittings wrote to say that he had been offered an empty rectory in Somerset as a place to work in during the Cambridge vacation, and asked if I would like to join him there. He had recently won the Chancellor's medal for poetry with *The Roman Road*, and the Oxford University Press was about to publish it together with a number of his shorter poems.

The rectory at Thorne St Margaret was a sizeable red-brick Victorian house, surrounded by a garden of thistles and nettles with straggling Dorothy Perkins roses surviving from better days. Tramps were said to make use of the downstair rooms, though none came while we were there. We borrowed two chairs and a table from the village hall, and slept on a couple of mattresses; mine, I remember, a thin cork-filled one, so narrow that I usually woke to find myself on the bare floor-boards where wood-lice took their early exercise. The shops at Wellington, visited on hired bicycles, provided a kettle, a saucepan, a teapot, a spirit-stove, and I suppose food, though I remember only a seven-pound tin of chocolate-coated digestive biscuits. A barrel of beer, which we broached and spigoted, was delivered to the door. These, with a shelfful of books, furnished the house. Of the books, the two things I most clearly remember reading were *The Waste Land* and *Tristram Shandy*.

Robert, when he had corrected the proofs of his poems, settled down to writing a play about Aesop and Rhodope, and encouraged me to try my hand at dramatising the tale of Aucassin and Nicolette. Each morning we walked across the fields to buy a newspaper from Mrs Boon; the day we looked forward to was the day of the week when Rebecca West wrote on the book page. Work was interrupted by a visit from Mary Taylor and two other girls who camped in a nearby field. Memory retains a supper, lobster and gin, eaten and drunk with them under a haystack.

There was an occasional morning service in the church, which had a peal of three ancient bells, one of them cracked. It had, like the strike of St Mary Woolnoth's, a dead sound on the final stroke. We made a pilgrimage or two; one to Alfoxden House where we did as the Wordsworths did in 1796, 'walked in the wood, a fine sunny morning'. On another day we cycled to the foot of the Quantocks, and by foot to Nether Stowey and Coleridge's cottage, passing on the way a gathering of gypsies speaking Romany. The Wellington monument on the Black Downs seen from the rectory window; the waxen pink stars of lesser centaury growing in the lanes; a linnet on a sumach tree— these are my heap of broken images.

If anything further is needed to speak for the validity of my claim, let me direct you to a little house called The Point, near Flushing, rising, it would seem, out of the rocks themselves. There my wife and I spent our honeymoon. The windows looked across the estuary to where the *Cutty Sark* rode at anchor. Now the *Cutty Sark* has docked for all time at Greenwich—we have made visits to her there—and it looks as though I shall end my days in Sussex. Seventy years of inconstancy to the West Country, no doubt, but my love for it never interrupted. I rest my case.

EDEN PHILLPOTTS

Widecombe Concert

This is the fiftieth chapter of *Widecombe Fair* (1913), one of the superb Dartmoor Cycle of novels by Eden Phillpotts (1862-1960). His comedy, *The Farmer's Wife* (1916), was suggested by scenes from the book, though Churdles Ash, the crusted retainer, crab-apple in Arcady, who rules the play, is not in the novel. (He had made a first appearance in *Sons of the Morning*, 1900.) Book and play stand apart from each other. Those who have met Phillpotts only on the stage should go to *Widecombe Fair* and read, say, Mary Hearn the postmistress's description of her visit to the new Exeter post-office, a passage that begins: 'There's no *news* in Exeter—it's all I complain of against it. A large and whirling city, no doubt, but there's never nothing *doing*, so far as I could see, like there is in Widecombe. A place of strangers; but the organs are very fine in the cathedral . . .'
The chapter we print below is practically self-contained. This is the narrative of the village concert, given on behalf of the blind and demanding Nicky Glubb (accordion-player) and his wife Nanny.

The schoolroom of the Church House was approached by a flight of steps in the rear of the building, and at the top of these, on the night of the Glubb concert, sat Birkett Johnson of Tunhill behind a little table. He sold the tickets, while within the schoolroom a couple of young women showed the people to their seats.

Nicky and his wife were the first to arrive, for she was now restored to health, and from their places near the door Nanny could mark the entrance and keep up a running account of the audience as it filtered in.

Flags were hung from the crossbeams of the roof, and a friend or two had sent green things to decorate the little stage. The lighting alone left anything to be desired. Twenty oil lamps hung from the walls, but many smoked, and threatened to make the atmosphere foul.

'Here come the Sweetlands!' said Nanny. 'They be all in the reserved shilling places—Mister and Misses, and that Harriet, his sister. They be in the third row from the front.'

The Glubbs wore their best clothes, and Nicky's accordion in its waterproof cover was under the seat of his chair.

'Who be they?' he asked, as feet shuffled past him and proceeded to the rear of the room.

'Four common people to the threp'my seats,' said Nanny. 'Sandy Blake, from Blackslade, and his wife and childer.'

He grew impatient.

'Why the hell don't they come in?' he asked, so loud that Mr Sweetland started in his chair, and looked round.

'Hush!' said Nanny, 'or you'll scare the folk. There's lots of time. The doors be only just opened.'

His keen ears detected the sound of wheels.

'There's a party come. I heard 'em,' he said.

'They be trooping in by legions now,' she answered. 'Here's Timothy Turtle and Sally and Pancras Widecombe from Ruggle-stone Inn; and here's they Gurneys from the Mill. I thought they'd be among the first—such pleasure loving folk as them. And if Nelly Gurney ban't with them! Seldom enough she goes junketing. They'm coming up to us.'

Abel Gurney and his wife, Sarah, stopped and shook hands with Nanny.

'Terrible glad you be saved alive, Mrs Glubb,' said the miller. ' 'Twould have been a great loss to us all, and to Nicky in particular, if you'd been called.'

'And looking pretty pert considering,' added Sarah. 'I'm sure I hope the people will cram the schoolroom afore the fun begins.'

'Is there to be programmes?' asked Abel Gurney.

'Proper printed programmes there's to be,' answered Nicky, 'and they damned boys ought to be running about selling 'em afore now. Twopence they are to cost, and they can be kept and put by for a remembrance.'

The Gurneys went to their places, and Nanny reported the arrival of four more people in the threepenny seats.

'And there's two in the sixpennies,' she said. 'They be Uncle Tom Cobleigh and his daughter, the widow.'

'Where did Turtle get to?' asked Nicky, and when he heard that the innkeeper and Sally were at the back of the room, he swore.

'Then I chuck him,' said Nicky; 'never again do I darken the doors of the Rugglestone. Proper decency did ought to have put the man in the bob seats. He shan't hear the last of that!'

'But you mind the nice things Mr Turtle sent while I was sick—and, be it as 'twill, there's a plenty going in the shilling seats. Here's Mr Gabriel Shillingford, and Miss Petronell, and Whitelock Smerdon, and Doctor Grenville—all in the bob places; and alongside them sit the Coplestone party from Southway—six of 'em! There's ten bob in a minute!'

'Be they boys nipping about with the programmes?' asked Mr Glubb; 'because if not, you run round to Johnson and tell him.'

'Pancras Widecombe have just started them,' answered Nanny. 'And here's quality! Squire and his missis and young Squire, and two more from Bag Park! They be seated next the Shillingfords, and Mr Shillingford have rose and bowed, and so have the doctor. There's a lot of handshaking going on, and every lesser eye be on 'em. The Squire's missis be slipping off a wonderful coat of fur—white wi' black tails on it. She's got a low gown on, and you can see to the dip in her bosom! And precious stones be flashing in her hair. 'Tis the colour of heather honey, and rises up on her head like a tower. And Squire and young Squire be in black and white, with glittering shirt-fronts and waistcoats open to the pit of their stomachs. And here come more sixpennies. If Jack Mogridge and his wife haven't gone in 'em! They're in black for that hanged man.'

'Be they Smerdons from Bone Hill come?'

'Not yet. But come they will for sartain—some of 'em. Here's the Hawkes—Old and Young, and Emma, and her eldest. They be all in the sixpennies.'

' 'Tis enough for them,' asserted Nicky, 'because the men be going to ring their bells as an item in the show. Get a programme and read it out to me.'

'Mrs Bowden's come in. Her husband no doubt made her come though he can't, because of a tissick in the chest.'

'So long as he paid for his seat, his chest don't matter,' declared Nicky.

'Here's old Bell!' cried Nanny. 'He's gone in a threp'my!'

'Has he? Well, I hope the varmint will like what I be going to say. 'Twill be out afore they can stop me.'

'He's sitting beside they Webbers, from Southcombe; and here be the proper Southcombe people—Mr Coaker and Mrs Coaker, and Miss Harvey and Elias. They be all bob folk in the second row; and Miss Harvey have catched sight of us, and be coming to speak.'

Tryphena joined Nicky and Nanny, and congratulated the latter on her appearance.

'It's going to be a perfectly splendid concert,' she said. 'All the shilling seats are sold, and more than half the sixpenny ones.'

'Here's the Vicar!' cried Nanny. 'He's gived orders for the windows to be oped, and Pancras Widecombe be telling him that if that's done the lamps will smoke, so 'tis a choice of evils. And Mr Brown's vexed about it, seemingly.'

'Fussy fool!' said Nicky. 'Who wants the windows opened? If us gets a bit fuggy, what's the odds? 'Twill only make it the more homelike. I'd let the men smoke as well as the lamps if I had my way.'

'Here's Mrs Reep, old Daniel's widow, along with the Smerdons Peter and Martha, and a few small fry. To the threp'my seats they go.'

Tryphena, perceiving that she was not wanted, returned to her aunt. She was going to recite a poem, and she felt very nervous. She had chosen Longfellow's 'Excelsior', and now sat and tried to concentrate her thoughts upon it.

Doctor Grenville came to talk to her.

'You and Petronell must come into the greenroom before the show begins,' he said. 'There's room for us all in there, and I've arranged for plenty of liquid refreshment. My conjuring pal from Exeter has arrived. He's making up. He always gives his show in costume. He's got some old Indian loot he puts on—full of secret pockets and things. I expect he'll be the hit of the evening—after your recitation.'

A hum of voices ascended in the schoolroom. The people arrived steadily and friends greeted each other and sat together and talked about their affairs.

'Here be Mary Hearn, stiff with pride, and her nose in the air,' said Nanny. 'And if she ban't seated next to the Sweetlands in the shilling seats! And here's Arthur Pierce, dressed like a gentleman, and here's Tom Gurney and his Mabel. They've met Pierce in the doorway, and all eyes be watching 'em. Arthur have got on black, and be wearing a red tie, and carrying his music to the manner born!'

'Look in the programme and see what 'tis the man be going to sing,' directed Nicky.

Nanny obeyed.

' "The Keys of Heaven", 'tis to be,' she said; 'and Pancras Widecombe is going to sing "The Heart Bowed Down".'

'Where do I come in?' asked Nicky.

'You be in item fourteen and last. 'Tis arranged you finish up, and then, after you've played and sung, you be going to make a speech and thank the people for me, and tell 'em how much the concert have fetched in. Birkett Johnson will have counted up the money by then.'

'I hope to God he won't make himself scarce with it, like that rip Christian Cobleigh and the Slate Club cash.'

'Not him. He ain't that sort.'

She read the programme through:

'No 1, Overture, piano and banjo, Miss Petronell Shillingford and Doctor Hugh Grenville. No 2, Recitation, "Betsy and I are out", by Mr Harold Harding.'

'Who be that?' asked Nicky. 'Never heard of the man.'

'He's a friend of the doctor's. Then No 3, Comic banjo song, "The Three Coons", by Doctor Hugh Grenville.'

'I wish he'd done a duet with me,' said Nicky. 'I could have told him some words from the old times that would properly have took the people's breath away, and set every female in the room blushing like a rose. And if Pierce weren't a fool, he'd sing something funny. Who wants "The Keys of Heaven" except of a Sunday? The keys of the beer barrel be more like it.'

'Mr Pierce comes next,' answered Nanny, 'he's No 4; and after him there's an item printed in extra big letters: "The Mysteries of the East, by Jam Jam-Jeeboy, the Nabob of Cochbangalee's own Juggler".'

'You can lead me out for a drink when that's going on,' declared Nicky. 'That's no good to me.'

'No 6 is Mr Pancras Widecombe, and a mournful song seemingly. What do he want to have a heart bowed down for? No 7 is the doctor again. This time playing a duet with Miss Shillingford. "Medley", 'tis called. Then comes the turn of the bell-ringers, and after them there's a comic recitation by that Harold Harding again: "The Fox that Lost His Tail", 'tis called: That's No 9 of the programme; No 10 comes next. 'Tis a piano piece by Miss Shillingford —all alone this time—Beet-hoven, 'tis.'

'Solemn and dull, no doubt,' said Nicky. 'What's the matter with this programme be that 'tis too deadly heavy. However, so long as the people have paid their money it don't matter; though there might be a few as would get nasty and ask for the stuff back again.'

'They never would do that,' declared Nanny. ' 'Tis for charity, and I be here for 'em to see 'tis genuine.'

'I'll do what I can at the finish,' promised Nicky. 'They've done one clever thing, and only one, so far as I can see, and that is they've kept the best for the last.'

'Miss Tryphena be No 11,' continued Nanny. 'A recitation again. "Excelsior", 'tis to be. These here foreign words won't please the people, I'm thinking, for they won't know what the mischief half of 'em stand for.'

'Whether or no, and whatever rubbish it may be, we must make a hell of a row after she's done, and lead the applause,' declared Mr Glubb. 'She's been a very sporting friend to us, and one good turn deserves another.'

'No 12 be they bell-ringers again,' concluded Mrs Glubb, 'and the Doctor is No 13.'

'Drat the man, what the mischief do we want with such a dose of him for?' asked Nicky.

'We must live and let live,' answered his wife. 'No doubt the young fellow thinks it be going to be a fine advertisement for his business.'

'Like his cheek if he do. 'Tis us as be going to be advertised, not him.'

'Well you'll come next and you'll give 'em a good bit of music, and tell 'em what money's been drawed in, and thank 'em from me. The room be getting nicely full now.'

Nicky did not answer, for he was full of thought. He had already conceived of a great and glorious outrage, and now he permitted the idea to mature in his brain.

The concert began, and the little company evinced its appreciation of the entertainment provided. The piano and banjo overture went well enough, save for the breaking of a banjo string, and the relations of the performers caused a sentimental sympathy with the effort.

But in the greenroom different emotions awakened, and the performers there assembled, in a scholastic atmosphere of slates, blackboards and scientific diagrams, could not fail to note that it was Tryphena Harvey, and not Petronell Shillingford, who engaged Doctor Grenville's chief attentions. He fussed over her continually, and exhibited a solicitousness for her anxieties in connection with 'Excelsior', that aroused curiosity and bred comment. Petronell was, of course, the first to observe it. Her pique took the form of a failure at the piano, while behind the scenes she devoted her attention to Mr Harold Harding, a long-haired railway-clerk from Newton Abbot, with yearnings towards the stage. His first recitation fell flat. The folk endured contentedly, however, and Petronell assured the artist afterwards that never had the familiar little drama been presented with more power and feeling. As a contrast came 'The Three Coons', presented by Doctor Grenville. He possessed no real sense of fun, but rolled his eyes and shouted and simulated facetiousness to the best of his power. The people laughed, and many who shared the singer's lack of humour appeared to be amused. Arthur Pierce, accompanied by Petronell Shillingford, sang 'The Keys of Heaven', in a high tenor, that broke to shrill falsetto. No critical faculty was brought to bear upon the song, but genuine amazement and admiration for the unsuspected audacity of the singer marked his hearers.

The Mysteries of the East by the Nabob of Cochbangalee's own Juggler introduced the person of an old Indian judge's son, who lived with his family at Exeter. This young man's face was painted brown. He wore a yellow turban with a glittering jewel upon it, and was attired in voluminous silken robes, rich in secret pockets and receptacles of all kinds. He was not, as he confessed afterwards, in his best form. Among other enchantments he produced many yards of pink tape from his mouth, burnt himself in an endeavour to eat fire, and failed to deceive his audience as to the whereabouts of an orange under three metal cups. Himself, however, he entirely bewildered in the course of this experiment.

Pancras Widecombe's mournful song failed absolutely, for, coming upon the doubtful triumph of the young man from Exeter, it found the audience in no mood for pathos. He had enemies, moreover, and the deadly weapon of laughter was directed against Pancras. Though he sang his best and bowed down his heart to the very depths of a guttural and bass despair, only a long-drawn chirrup and cricket-like stridulation of merriment greeted him.

' 'Tis the fool's face, not what he be singing, that makes me laugh,' confessed the elder Coaker, who was much amused. 'When you think upon Widecombe, and his ever-green conceit of hisself, and his calm cheek at all times, to see him pretending to be sad and sat upon! He ought to have sung, "I'm master of all I survey", or some such stuff.'

Few but Sally Turtle regarded Pancras with much more than laughter, and he displayed his emotion in a red face and scowling expression as he withdrew.

'For two pins, I'd have told 'em they was a lot of ill-behaved clod-poles, as didn't know a beautiful song when they heard it,' he declared to Young Harry Hawke, with a panting bosom, in the greenroom. But Young Harry loved him not, and only grinned in his face.

'How was they to know the song was beautiful?' he answered. 'You ought to have told 'em afore you began.'

Doctor Grenville and Petronell appeared again together in a duet, and since behind the scenes his betrothed was feeling angry and jealous, she did herself small justice before the footlights. Thrice she lost the time. It was a stammering and hesitating achievement, and the fault rested with Petronell. They did not speak to each other when they came off the stage, and neither appeared to bow an acknowledgement of the applause.

Mr Harding next recited, and his performance was spoiled by the tragical collapse of a Smerdon girl. She fainted and was borne out to a bench in the passage, where Doctor Grenville protested audibly at the Smerdon girl's tight lacing, and ruined the secret joy of her young life—a pair of corsets for which she had 'saved up' through many weeks. When she came to her senses, her armour spread in tatters beneath her bosom, and she wept and crept homewards harbouring the saddest thoughts.

Behind the scenes, presently, Petronell told Hugh Grenville that she did not wish him to turn over the pages of her Beethoven's 'Farewell to the Piano'; but the doctor protested.

'What'll your father and everybody think?' he asked. 'They'll say we've quarrelled.'

She was firm, and Mr Harding consented to perform the task. Petronell played well on this occasion, but was glad to be done with her part of a painful evening. She stayed only to hear Tryphena, very white and nervous, enter upon the recitation from Longfellow, and then she departed, bearing through the night a sorrow even deeper than that of the Smerdon girl. For she, poor maiden, found tears relieve her on the way home to Bone Hill; but Petronell's eyes mirrored the nightly stars without a tremor.

Tryphena stumbled to the end of 'Excelsior', forgetting every inflexion and gesture that Doctor Grenville had been at pains to teach her; but the affection of her friends took the form of hand-clapping and stamping. Nicky and Nanny led the noise, and continued long after everybody else was silent.

The subsequent bell-ringing was a familiar entertainment, and excited no great attention, while upon Doctor Grenville's reappearance it seemed the audience began to feel with Nicky Glubb that it was possible to have enough, if not too much of him. Not one encore had marked the concert—an unusual circumstance; but the entertainment, indeed, proceeded at low level, and few loopholes for enthusiasm were offered even to the most amiable. The general sense of the company seemed to indicate a stern duty meritoriously performed by all present—performers and audience alike.

Then Nicky came forward, led by his wife. She carried his accordion and put it into his hand when he reached the platform. The greenroom was now deserted, and the other performers had entered the schoolroom to hear the financial result of their efforts. The sum was whispered to Mrs Glubb by Birkett Johnson, as she ascended to the stage.

The blind man played and sang while the people rose and helped each other into coats and wraps. There was a sound of wheels through the night, and the speech of drivers without.

Nicky gave two songs and made the most of them, while the accordion volleyed and thundered an accompaniment. Then his wife led him to the footlights.

'Ladies and gentlemen,' he said. 'You be gathered here tonight to help a blind man and his wife, and specially her—because she's just fought a fearful battle with Death, and come out of the Valley of the Shadow a shadow herself. The sum that you've gived in among you for this evening's concert, such as it was, be six pound, eighteen shilling, and sixpence, including a bit for the programmes; and me and my wife thank you with all our hearts for your great goodness. And we thank all the kind people who have done their poor bestest to amuse the company this evening. And the money will help to keep me and Nanny out of the almshouse for many and many a day—where beastly, useless, old dogs like Bell be chained up; though such dregs did ought to be knocked on the head once for all in my opinion! And I hope the swine will soon be wriggling in a place as rhymes with his name!'

'Hush! Hush! Take him away! Shame on you, Glubb!' shouted reproving voices, and Nicky, grinning his well-known horrible smile, shuffled off holding Nanny's hand. Many hissed him for this assault, but he cared not.

Then into the night streamed the people, and swiftly they vanished, some driving and some walking through the darkness. The real pleasure of that evening's work circled round fifty supper-tables, where the unconscious humours of the concert were weighed and measured to accompaniment of laughter both deep and shrill.

JOHN PRINCE

Terror at Widecombe

John Prince (1642–1723) was Vicar of Berry-Pomeroy for forty-two years. In 1701 he published what he called, comprehensively, '*The Worthies of Devon:* A work whereon the lives and fortunes of the Most Famous Divines, Statesmen, Swordsmen, Physicians, Writers, and other Eminent Persons, natives of that most noble province, from before the Norman Conquest down to the present age, are memorized, in an alphabetical order, out of the most approved authors, both in print and manuscript. In which an account is given, not only of divers very deserving persons (many of which were never hitherto made publick) but of several antient and noble families; their seats and habitations; the distance they bear to the next great town; their coats of arms fairly cut, with other things, no less profitable, than pleasant and delightful.' One of the subjects was the Rev George Lyde, of Widecombe-in-the-Moor.

Lyde, George, was born at Loventor, a clean and handsome seat, in the parish of Berry-Pomeroy, about three miles east of Totnes in this county, of honest and gentile parents. He was the sixth of ten sons, every one of which had no less than five sisters; and being of a towardly genius, he was continued at school until he was well fitted for the university. After which he was placed into Baliol-College in Oxford, where he continued a diligent student, until such time as he had compleated his degrees of arts; and then retiring into his native country, he took holy orders, and was preferred to the vicarige of Wythecombe or Wydecombe (Widecombe) in the Moor; so called at least for its joyning to, if not its standing in, the south part of the so famous forrest of Dartmoor, in this county. Where he continued a laborious preacher and a prudent pastor unto a good old age.

In this reverend vicar's time it was (the chief ground of my inserting him here) that that most memorable instance of a dreadful Providence happened in his church of Wydecombe, in the very act of his celebrating the service of God there; at which time he behaved himself with that courage and bravery, as became an officer under the great Captain of our Salvation in his church-militant. The whole transaction being so exceeding true and wonderful, I also shall endeavour to transmit the memory thereof down to posterity.

In the year of our Lord 1638, Oct 21, being Sunday, and the congregation being gathered together in the parish church of Wydecombe, in the afternoon in service time, there happened a very great darkness, which still encreased to that degree, that they could not see to read: Soon after, a terrible and fearful thunder was heard, like the noise of many great guns, accompanied with dreadful lightning, to the great amazement of the people; the darkness still encreasing that they could not see each other; when there presently came such an extraordinary flame of lightning as filled the church with fire, smoak, and a loathsome smell like brimstone; a ball of fire came in likewise at the window, and passed thro' the church, which so affrighted the congregation, that most of them fell down in their seats, some upon their knees, others on their faces, and some one upon another, crying out of burning and scalding, and all giving up themselves up for dead.

This our Mr George Lyde was in his pulpit, and altho' much astonished, yet thro' Divine mercy, had no harm: But was a sad spectator of the hurt and sufferings of others, the lightning seizing on his wife and burning her cloaths and many parts of her body, and another gentlewoman by her in the same manner; but her maid and child sitting at the pew door had no hurt; another woman attempting to run out of the church, had her cloaths set on fire, and was so miserably scorch'd and burn'd that she died the same night. One Mr Mead had his head suddainly struck against the wall in his seat with such violence, that he also died the same night, no other hurt being observed, his son setting by him had no harm. At the same instant, another man had his head cloven, his skull wrent into three pieces, and his brains thrown upon the ground whole; but the hair of his head, thro' the violence of the blow, stuck fast to a pillar near him, where it remained a woful spectacle a long while after. Some seats in the body of the church were turned upside down, yet those who sate in them had little or no hurt. One man going out of the chancel-door, his dog ran before him, who was whirled about toward the door and fell down stark dead, upon which the master stepped back and was preserved.

The church itself was much torn and defaced with the thunder and lightning; a beam whereof breaking in the midst, fell down between the minister and clerk, and hurt neither: The steeple was much wrent; and it was observed where the church was most torn, there the least hurt was done among the people. There was none hurted with the timber or stone, but one maid, who, it was judged, was killed by the fall of a stone; which might easily happen, since stones were thrown down from the steeple as fast as if it had been by a hundred men.

A pinacle of the tower being thrown down, beat thro' into the church: The pillar against which the pulpit stood, being newly whited, was turned black and sulphury. There were in all four persons killed, and sixty-two hurt, divers of them having their linen burnt, tho' their outward garments were not so much as singed. The lightning being passed, and the people in a terrible 'maze, a gentleman in the town stood up and said, 'Neighbours, in the name of God, shall we venture out of the church?' To whom Mr Lyde, the minister, answered, 'Let us make an end with prayer, for it is better to die here than in another place.' But the people looking about them, and seeing the church so terribly wrent and torn over their heads, durst not proceed in the publick devotions, but went out of the church; and at the same time the Bowling Alley, near the church-yard, was turned into pits and heaps, as if it had been plowed.

This story several yet living are able to attest the truth of; which being so strange and unusual an act of Providence, I shall here crave the reader's pardon to inquire in to a few circumstances relating to occurrences of this kind. . . The cause may be considered two ways, either according to philosophy or divinity.

1 The natural and philosophical cause of such devastations, is thunder and lightning; not thunder (which spends itself chiefly in noise) so much as lightning, which however soft and lambent it may seem to be, is yet of that resistless force and power, where it meets opposition, that it often overturns sturdy oaks, lofty citadels, yea! and the firmest mountains themselves. . . If any should wonder how it should lighten so much (as often it does) in violent rains; things mixed with and compounded of niter, sulphur, calxviva, and bitumen, may be enkindled by an aspertion of water. We have a clear demonstration hereof, in that which the chymists call phosphorus.

2 As to the theological cause, that is very often the wrath and justice of Almighty God; for 'tis certain, what one truly observes, such dreadful thunders and lightnings don't arise by chance, or the meer motion of matter, nor ought to be referred to pure natural causes; but are sometime produced by the immediate direction of Almighty God; and He may permit evil spirits, who have un-doubtedly a great power in the air, their chieftain, in Holy Scripture, being called 'The Prince of the Power of the Air' to raise storms and tempests, and to scatter abroad thunders and lightnings, to mischief what they can the children of men, whose happiness they have envied since they fell from their own. . . Though the holy angels are often the ministers of God's grace and benefaction to the world, yet we doubt not but that He uses the evil ones as His beadles and lictors, to execute His wrath upon the children of disobedience . . .

The pious people of this parish (their church being at length repaired) hung up therein, in a votive table for that purpose ordained, a grateful memorial of this wonderful Providence; induced hereunto by that of the Psalmist, quoted in the title of it, 'The merciful and gracious Lord hath so done His marvellous works, that they ought to be had in remembrance.' Wherein is contained a brief history of what then happened, in large verse, consisting of seven feet, too tedious to be here inserted, though they thus begin:

In token of our thanks to God this table is erected,
Who in a dreadful thunderstorm our persons then protected.

These were written by one Mr Hill of this parish, gent, who was present when this tempest happened.

Mr Lyde (of whom we have been discoursing) wrote also a large copy of verses on this occasion, in English hexameter (a transcript whereof I have by me) . . . They are too many to be hereunto subjoyned, but they thus conclude:

> Oh! bless'd be God! for ever bless His name!
> Which hath preserv'd us from that burning flame!
> Oh! Let the voice of Praise be heard as loud,
> As was the thunder breaking through the cloud.
> Oh! Let the fire of our devotion flame
> As high as heaven, pierce the celestial frame, &c.

Mr Lyde, whom God was pleased thus wonderfully to preserve, lived many years after this, even beyond the Restauration of the church and of the King, Char 2d; and being full of days, he exchanged this painful life for (we hope) a blessed immortality, AD 1673, and lies interred in the chancel of his church at Wyde-combe, without any sepulchral monument.

A. L. ROWSE

St Carroc's Crucifix

Dr A.L. Rowse, Fellow of All Souls and internationally honoured historian (*Tudor Cornwall* is one book of many), is also eminent as Shakespearian scholar, poet, autobiographer, and writer on many themes. In *St Carroc's Crucifix* he is a storyteller.

St Carroc's was a most inaccessible place. How well I had reason to think so, I thought, when I paid my first visit to the young man taking possession. I had received an alarming paper of instructions how to get there. I was to make for St Greep Church on the other side of the River Fowey. Now the Other Side of the River Fowey is a no-man's-land, where anything may happen. Beguilingly beautiful, but terrifyingly steep lanes where nothing can pass—except ghosts—roads that lead down to dead-ends by innumerable creeks.

I had to make for the metropolis of Lerryn, capital of the neighbourhood. I passed through the pretty village, with its pink-and-white-washed houses, its rivercraft, and over the hump of the bridge, one Sunday evening in the depth of the Cornish summer. The place was almost blotted out by blustering wind and rain. Fuchsias and blue hydrangeas strained at the leash like demented animals; the rain merged with the water in the creek overflowing at full floodtide.

Through the village, I took a turn off the main road up a steep narrow lane to the promised beacon of St Greep. Apprehensive as always in this country—for how could I reverse all the way down that twisting lane if I met anything?—I pushed on up, trumpeting at every corner like the coming of the Lord.

St Greep Church passed in a storm of rain: the time of evensong, not a soul visible, but a burst of a solitary bell suddenly clashed into the car and was gone. On I went until the road forked. I was to ignore the ironic notice 'One Way Street', go flat against it, down into and through a farm area and make a sharp left turn.

I obeyed, made a left turn: here was a renovated house with back-court of slate—should I follow the cart-track to the left? I looked, just in time, to see a precipice and the green sheet of water of the submerged creek before me. I asked my whereabouts of two upstanding youths, bareheaded in rain and wind, with something suggestively Arthurian about them. One was tall and black-haired, hair standing up straight and short-cropped; the other a fair Sir Galahad. The dark one took the lead and answered me with a foreign accent.

Backing away from the precipice, I made along the top of the creek to the recognisable declivity on the left, a white gate left open for me and into the quiet of the enchanted valley-bottom; a range of ancient farm-buildings; stones of the old monastic cell and chapel. I jolted along the rough drive to the Queen Anne farm-house facing the head of the creek, the sodden lawn and, beyond, the Monks' Walk along the edge of the moss-green water.

There on the steps in the rain, mackintosh huddled round shoulders, was the owner to greet me.

New to the place, he had already developed a fixation upon it (or had it upon him?). St Carroc's had got him. His inheritance of it was characteristically deviant, in the Cornish manner. In the Victorian Age there had been two illegitimate descents in succession, the whole place going down gradually, outlying bits of land sold off, until only the valley-bottom was left, the house with its river-frontage and its memories.

Gawen was the last sprig of the old stock, a branch that had gone out to New Zealand in early days. Himself a promising young painter in London now, he had scraped together every penny to save the place from going out of the family at the end of the feckless line there.

Everything was to do. He couldn't afford to come down for more than a week or two, or a weekend, at a time; now he was anxious to show me what he had accomplished. Up over the rocky steps we went, into the back-court with the debris that had come to light from the monastic cell. Every scrap was precious to this passionate artist from so far away, whose deeper roots were nevertheless here. I glimpsed a holy-water stoup of rough granite, a bit of column with its capital that went back to Norman times. Various other bits and pieces were lying about; a shaped mullion, the head of a medieval or Tudor window—all precious as jewels to this denizen of a newer world—the Long Cloud on the fringes of the Pacific.

We went inside. Gawen explained his plans. The dairy was to become the kitchen, the kitchen to become the dining-room, screened off like a medieval hall. In the staircase-hall one could see that the house had been built for a family of gentlefolk; the staircase had style; wide-spread stairs with good low treads, twisting balusters carrying up to a spacious landing. On either side was a parlour, one with a painted corner-cupboard, which Gawen had had copied for the hall. He had already completed the decoration of his front room, doing the painting himself.

He had gathered a great armful of foliage and flowers to take back with him to London. I was surprised at his going to so much trouble.

'I can't bear to leave the place,' he said. 'It's always like this when I'm going.'

He hadn't been off the premises the whole week he had been there. Out of doors he had been scything and mowing and weeding, carrying hay and burning up rubbish, seeing to the boat moored by the Monks' Walk; indoors he had been painting and furbishing, all on his own. He clearly needed someone to help him.

There he stood, six feet of him, tall and slender, rather lank dark hair, a curiously low voice with a tang of accent more colonial than Cornish. An appealing personality, not easy to penetrate, rather lonely this melancholy summer evening—and himself sad at leaving. Decidedly, he needed a helping hand.

'Do you know the story of the crucifix that was found here, turned up in the soil like those carved stones at the door? I'm very anxious to see it. Wouldn't it be wonderful if it came back to where it belongs?'

I promised to look it up and tell him what I could find out at our next meeting. Myself away all winter in California, it was not until the next summer that we coincided in Cornwall again and I was able to tell him what I had learned.

The monastic cell—never more than a prior and a couple of monks there all through the Middle Ages, more often a prior with one young monk—had been founded by Robert of Mortain, half-brother of the Conqueror, who got the earldom of Cornwall at the Conquest and gave the cell to the abbey of Mont St Michel in Normandy.

Of course, the place went far back beyond the Normans to Celtic days and the Age of the Saints. Its origin was the holy well, a little way up the slope, a damp spot in Gawen's orchard. At the head of the creek the saint and his disciples had erected a stone cross now in St Greep churchyard, removed in the Victorian Age. Around it in succeeding ages were buried his faithful successors, Celtic hermits and medieval monks, under what is now Gawen's innocent front lawn, smooth and shaven.

Laurence Castletown was the last prior, accompanied to the end by his companion, a younger monk, James. Except for saying mass, hearing confessions, keeping the light before the saint going —they were really a couple of farmers living off the soil like everyone else.

Mute and inglorious as their lives had been, they were not going to see the end of all that century-long way of life without making their mute inglorious protest. When the monasteries were suppressed and sentence of expulsion passed upon the prior and his companion, they took the most cherished possession of their chapel, the gilt crucifix that stood on the desecrated altar, and buried it at night deep in the corner of the garth.

I have seen the crucifix, and a treasure it is—even if only of copper-gilt. It looked to me, on the sole occasion when I was allowed to see it, to be of the thirteenth century or early fourteenth when the great John de Grandison came from the Papal Court at

Avignon to be Bishop of Exeter and was a connoisseur of such things. It had an almost Spanish look—that deep Spanish sadness in the elongated face, the emaciation of the body. The early date of the work spoke in the flat treatment of the toes, the fingers of the outstretched hands.

What would I not give to possess this treasure, yielded up by the earth after some three hundred and fifty years of oblivion?

If this was how I felt about it, what would not Gawen feel about it when he saw it?

It had been dug up in the 1880s, in the corner where it had been buried in the 1530s. The farmer had been glad to part with it to the local landowner, a man of antiquarian tastes who appreciated it. It was now in the possession of his granddaughter, Fay Morgan, who had once let me see it.

Gawen, of course, was pining to get a glimpse of it.

I did not see him again for a year, and in the interval two developments had taken place.

Gawen's painting had flowered, he had found his own style and was beginning to be successful. He had discovered the means of expressing his own inner fantasy, his passion for the spirit of place, the life that houses live on their own when no one is looking, especially deserted houses where much has happened—one longs to know what—and of rendering their atmosphere. He had an exquisite sense of colour and line: he was a colourist and a *fantaisiste*.

Gawen had found himself, and his own true nature, in his work. He would be able to live more at St Carroc's.

And, besides, a much-needed helper had come to his aid there. Diego, the dark young Spaniard who had directed me on my first visit, had descended the hillside to take a hand in the operations that were too much for Gawen on his own. He was not only a good hand with a scythe but with a boat; like his namesake, the apostle, he was a fisherman—expert at hoiking up trout from the river, or eels from the creek, and as expertly baking them. He was a good cook—which Gawen was not.

Diego developed a fixation on St Carroc's; it spoke to him as it spoke to Gawen. A native of Galicia, indeed of Santiago itself, Diego was of the same stock as the Cornish, dark, by turns melancholy and gay; above all, of the soil.

Meanwhile, what of the crucifix? How was Gawen to come by that?

He would have to make love to the aloof daughter of the lord of the manor. In a world falling all round her, she was rather up-stage. Would he make a good impression?

Apparently he did, for she too was interested in the arts. She was only a year or two older than Gawen, and heart-free, her husband having been killed in the war. But she was not easy to please; and she was not giving herself away. Moreover, she possessed what Gawen very much wanted—the crucifix that belonged to St Carroc's.

There was some difficulty in bringing them together; but the lady came one afternoon to picnic on the lawn in front of the creek. She came up the river alone, herself at the wheel of her motor-boat, painted green, the colour of the creek. The effect was striking; she was wearing a light green summer-dress; it seemed as if this vision arose from the water itself.

I had been asked to tea, and was suitably impressed by the elegance of her appearance. She was tiny, like a fairy-tale princess; but such was her poise, the curve of foot and instep, that she lost nothing in seductiveness or, more curiously, authority as she took possession of the lawn.

Diego moved about noiselessly, bringing the tea, handing the anchovies of his native Galicia. I, of course, was a mere foil.

She was talking to Gawen about the paintings at the Hall. (It was called 'Hall', as rarely in Cornwall: and was more like a Gothic castle out of Horace Walpole or Mrs Radcliffe.)

'You really must come and see the paintings one day—both of you.' It was kind of her to include me—she evidently meant me; but Diego was as clearly omitted.

'You know that Opie, before he left Cornwall, was taken up by my family. We've got several of his early paintings—two moonlight scenes by the sea-shore. Where do you suppose he can have got the idea?—an uninstructed peasant painting on his own down here in Cornwall. He can never have heard of Vernet, can he?'

'I don't suppose so. But his friend, Dr Wolcot, might well have had engravings. He was an amateur painter himself.'

'Oh, the horrid Peter Pindar, with his ballads against the ladies of Fowey!'

The conversation moved to another painter of moonlight scenes, the much less well known Patch.

Gawen had never heard of him.

The lady had. 'Didn't he have to live abroad for the good of his country?' she said disapprovingly, taking us all in at a glance.

I helped Diego to carry the tea-things in, while Gawen demonstrated the Monks' Walk with its rare ferns to its rarer visitor. In the encouraging atmosphere of that green cloister he was able to raise the question of the crucifix and whether it might be allowed to revisit its old home too. The lady promised that she would bring it with her on her next visit.

I watched her departure, the vision melting into the water, one with the creek. 'Morgan le Fay,' I registered.

I was not present on her second visit, neither was Diego. So it was not clear whether she succeeded in penetrating Gawen's defence, or to what extent, for something upset him and disturbed the peace of mind he needed for his work.

The lady had broken her word to bring the crucifix with her; and Gawen's disturbance of mind had something to do with that. The crucifix had become a symbol of the subterranean tension that had risen up between them. She had certainly managed to disturb the still waters of the creek.

On one side he was tempted; but was she desirable in herself?

Yes—oddly so. There was the fairy princess, smiling, intelligent, slightly mocking—out to seduce. She was very dark; black hair, with a rare tinge of rust in it. Her eyes seemed dark; they were certainly brown, but if you dared to look closer you saw that they belonged to the kind that have as much green as brown, a certain witchery. (Was she a witch, perhaps?)

Other things suggested themselves: an easy way of life, no more scuffling like the gulls in the creek for the garbage of critics' notice. She had possessions to offer, beautiful objects— the Hall was full of them. (Would there, however, be a way of escape?) The joys of family life—would they turn out to be so?

A choice was posed—a choice between two ways of life. He could only decide for himself; no one could help him—at least no other human being. Something else came to his aid.

The crucifix came back to St Carroc's.

On her third visit, her third time of asking, the lady brought it with her. Perhaps she thought it would settle the issue—as, in the end, it did.

Gawen's eyes were filled with desire when, for the first time, he came face to face with it. But it was an unexpected, a strange, confrontation. Looking at it closely, taking the cold object into his warm hands, enfolding it, he ceased to want to possess it.

What he found was that, gazing at the weary lids of those half-closed eyes, the Oriental-looking slit of suffering beneath them, he himself was enabled to see more clearly. He saw himself as he was, accepted himself as he was, came to terms with himself.

He saw that renunciation was the path to fulfilment—renunciation of anything that distracted him from his work, however alluring or seductive, or whatever it promised. It was not all renunciation: he could enjoy those delights that were propitious to creation, whatever anyone else might think. He was not to live his life in the light of others' eyes.

He took a last look into hers—and saw that in their depths there was a gleam of red. A warning of danger? A suggestion of resentment, an affronted pride? Was she altogether human?

He looked at the downcast eyes of the figure on the cross—patience and suffering, a willed resignation to his own fate, not in accordance with another's will.

He hesitated no longer. In that moment the lady saw herself defeated.

Without a word she withdrew, like a ghost, from the house. The moon had come up over the creek; the tide was at the full, lapping at the Monks' Walk.

As she drew away in her boat, under the witchery of the moon-laced trees, she took a dark object from her breast, held it for a moment in full sight of the house, then threw it into the shadowy waters.

It glistened in the moonlight for a flash as it fell, and Gawen knew that he was free.

Here, in South Devon, across the mouth of the river Dart, looking from Dartmouth, is Kingswear on the eastern bank. Dartmouth was once a major port, guarded by castles on each side of the harbour mouth. Dame Agatha Christie lived not far up-river at Greenway House.

The North Cliff above the magnificent Valley of the Rocks, with its immense piled stones, near Lynmouth in North Devon. The poet Coleridge, who brought the Wordsworths to see it, paid for the outing by writing 'The Ancient Mariner'.

This tinted etching shows Exeter High Street in 1942. The church is St Lawrence, and it was destroyed in the Blitz. The picture is by P.V. Pitman, an Exeter artist.

'I was always delighted with the melancholy grandeur of a sea-shore.' The writer is John Constable (1776–1832); his oil painting of Weymouth Bay, now in the National Gallery and here reproduced, has been called 'one of the great documents of nineteenth-century naturalistic painting, a major work by any standard'. It dates from about 1816, Constable's honeymoon in Dorset.

'There runs between Lyme Regis and Axmouth six miles to the west, one of the strangest coastal landscapes in Southern England.' So John Fowles begins a chapter from *The French Lieutenant's Woman*. The steep Undercliff, solitary, wild, and chasm-split, is 'really the mile-long slope caused by the erosion of the ancient vertical cliff-face . . .'

No railway is more 'scenic', or more loved, than the present Western line, originally planned by Brunel, which runs through the sandstone tunnels and by the sea at Dawlish, with only a sea wall between it and the beach. This painting shows a landslip on what was then the South Devon Railway, near Parson's Tunnel, in 1852.

Gorran Haven, where so many fishermen and deep-water sailors have been bred through the centuries, is quiet round its harbour: a part of essential Cornwall, today's as well as of older generations. A poet celebrated: 'I did not know them, but I knew their sea/ Its pelting flourish by the granite quay.'

The lych-gate of the splendid church of St Pancras at Widecombe-in-the-Moor, the Dartmoor village which—according to folk-song—Uncle Tom Cobleigh, Bill Brewer, Jan Stewer, and the rest, visited at the September fair. Eden Phillpotts's novel, *Widecombe Fair,* from which a chapter appears in this book (see page 66) is set in the village.

There are fantastic rocks at Bedruthan Steps on the north coast of Cornwall. Time and the weather have moulded them into such shapes as this in the picture. An 1889 guide-book noted 'gigantic confusion mingled with the most peaceful beauty'.

'The Hoe, Plymouth' by J.M.W. Turner (c1825–9). Immediately below the dancers and the cheerfully boisterous crowd in the foreground is Cattewater, leading to Sutton Pool, hidden on the left; the Citadel on Plymouth Hoe is down to the right.

A rood screen separates the chancel of a church from the nave. This beautiful example, gilt and coloured and with saints painted on its lower panels, dates from the early fifteenth century and is in the hamlet of Torbryan, near Newton Abbot. During the Commonwealth the rector preserved his screen by whitewashing it.

Among the glistening serpentine rocks of Kynance Cove, in the far south of Cornwall, Tennyson on his 1848 tour saw the 'glorious grass-green monsters of waves' and went into the 'caves of Asparagus Island' (in centre of photograph). Behind is The Rill from which the Spanish Armada was sighted in July 1588.

This beach, Little Perhaver, is in the litany of beaches, coves and havens that the
Cornish writer, Anne Treneer, who was born in the remoteness of Gorran, named
in her autobiography, *School House in the Wind:* 'Hemmick, Gorran Haven, with
Perhaver and Little Perhaver; Porthluney, East and West Portholland . . .'

JANE AUSTEN

Louisa on the Cobb

Lyme Regis, in Dorset, is a few hundred yards east of the Devon border. The Cobb is a two-levelled harbour breakwater. Here, in *Persuasion* (1818), Jane Austen's last completed novel, published posthumously, Louisa Musgrove has her fall. When Alfred Tennyson visited Lyme in 1867, lured by the passage in *Persuasion*, he walked nine miles from Bridport and, calling on Francis Turner Palgrave, said at once, refusing all refreshment: 'Now take me to the Cobb and show me the steps from which Louisa Musgrove fell.'

The fall is a piece of dramatic action rare in an Austen novel; another rarity is such a long descriptive passage as that about Lyme. Here the period is just after the Napoleonic wars when naval officers have leisure, and prize money, to enjoy country life. Captain Harville, who had been severely wounded, is spending the winter at Lyme. Captain Wentworth, an old friend staying with his sister not far away, comes over to see Harville with some of the young people he has met, among them gentle Anne Elliot, rather older than the Musgrove girls of Uppercross, Louisa and Henrietta. There are also Louisa's brother Charles and his wife Mary. Captain Benwick is staying with the Harvilles.

Anne had known Wentworth some years before, but what might have been a marriage failed to come about. She is silently pained as she watches the growing devotion between Louisa and Wentworth. Louisa's injury serves the plot as it prolongs the estrangement between Wentworth and Anne.

The young people were all wild to see Lyme . . . though November, the weather was by no means bad; and, in short, Louisa, who was the most eager of the eager, having formed the resolution to go, and besides the pleasure of doing as she liked, being now armed with the idea of merit in maintaining her own way, bore down all the wishes of her father and mother for putting it off till summer; and to Lyme they were to go—Charles, Mary, Anne, Henrietta, Louisa, and Captain Wentworth.

The first heedless scheme had been to go in the morning and return at night, but to do this Mr Musgrove, for the sake of his horses, would not consent; and when it came to be rationally considered, a day in the middle of November would not leave much time for seeing a new place, after deducting seven hours, as the nature of the country required, for going and returning. They were, consequently, to stay the night there, and not to be expected back till the next day's dinner. This was felt to be a considerable amendment; and though they all met at the Great House at rather an early breakfast hour, and set off very punctually, it was so much past noon before the two carriages, Mr Musgrove's coach containing the four ladies, and Charles's curricle, in which he drove Captain Wentworth, were descending the long hill into Lyme, and entering upon the still steeper street of the town itself, that it was very evident that they would not have more than time for looking about them, before the light and warmth of the day were gone.

After securing accommodations, and ordering a dinner at one of the inns, the next thing to be done was unquestionably to walk directly down to the sea. They were come too late in the year for any amusement or variety which Lyme, as a public place, might offer; the rooms were shut up, the lodgers almost gone, scarcely any family but of the residents left—and, as there is nothing to admire in the buildings themselves, the remarkable situation of the town, the principal street almost hurrying into the water, the walk to the Cobb, skirting round the pleasant little bay, which in the season is animated with bathing machines and company, the Cobb itself, its old wonders and new improvements, with the very beautiful line of cliffs stretching out to the east of the town, are what the stranger's eye will seek; and a very strange stranger it must be, who does not see charms in the immediate environs of

Lyme, to make him wish to know it better. The scenes in its neighbourhood, Charmouth, with its high grounds and extensive sweeps of country, and still more, its sweet retired bay, backed by dark cliffs, where fragments of low rock make it the happiest spot for watching the flow of the tide, for sitting in unwearied contemplation;—the wooded varieties of the cheerful village of Up Lyme, and, above all, Pinny, with its green chasms between romantic rocks, where the scattered forest trees and orchards of luxuriant growth declare that many a generation must have passed away since the first partial falling of the cliff prepared the ground for such a state, where a scene so wonderful and so lovely is exhibited, as may more than equal any of the resembling scenes of the far-famed Isle of Wight: these places must be visited, and visited again, to make the worth of Lyme understood.

The party from Uppercross, passing down by the now deserted and melancholy-looking rooms, and still descending, soon found themselves on the sea-shore, and lingering only, as all must linger and gaze on a first return to the sea, who ever deserve to look on it at all, proceeded towards the Cobb, equally their object in itself and on Captain Wentworth's account; for in a small house, near the foot of an old pier of unknown date, were the Harvilles settled. Captain Wentworth turned in to call on his friend; the others walked on, and he was to join them on the Cobb . . .

[Before going home next day there was a final walk along the Cobb.]

. . . There was such a general wish to walk along it once more, all were so inclined, and Louisa soon grew so determined, that the difference of a quarter of an hour, it was found, would be no difference at all, so with all the kind leave-taking, and all the kind interchange of invitations and promises which may be imagined, they parted from Captain and Mrs Harville at their own door, and still accompanied by Captain Benwick, who seemed to cling to them to the last, proceeded to make the proper adieus to the Cobb . . .

There was too much wind to make the high part of the new Cobb pleasant for the ladies, and they agreed to get down the steps to the lower, and all were contented to pass quietly and carefully down the steep flight, excepting Louisa; she must be jumped down them by Captain Wentworth. In all their walks, he had had to jump her from the stiles; the sensation was delightful to her. The hardness of the pavement for her feet made him less willing upon the present occasion; he did it, however; she was safely down, and instantly, to show her enjoyment, ran up the steps to be jumped down again. He advised her against it, thought the jar too great; but no, he reasoned and talked in vain; she smiled and said, 'I am determined I will;' he put out his hands; she was too precipitate by half a second, she fell on the pavement on the Lower Cobb, and was taken up lifeless!

There was no wound, no blood, no visible bruise; but her eyes were closed, she breathed not, her face was like death.—The horror of that moment to all who stood around!

Captain Wentworth, who had caught her up, knelt with her in his arms, looking on her with a face as pallid as her own, in an agony of silence. 'She is dead! she is dead!' screamed Mary, catching hold of her husband, and contributing with his own horror to make him immovable; and in another moment, Henrietta, sinking under the conviction, lost her senses too, and would have fallen on the steps, but for Captain Benwick and Anne, who caught and supported her between them.

'Is there no one to help me?' were the first words which burst from Captain Wentworth, in a tone of despair, and as if all his own strength were gone.

'Go to him, go to him,' cried Anne, 'for heaven's sake go to him. I can support her myself. Leave me, and go to him. Rub her hands, rub her temples; here are salts—take them, take them.'

Captain Benwick obeyed, and Charles at the same moment, disengaging himself from his wife, they were both with him; and Louisa was raised up and supported more firmly between them, and every thing was done that Anne had prompted, but in vain; while Captain Wentworth, staggering against the wall for his support, exclaimed in the bitterest agony,

'Oh God! her father and mother!'

'A surgeon!' said Anne.

He caught the word; it seemed to rouse him at once, and saying only, 'True, true, a surgeon this instant,' was darting away, when Anne eagerly suggested,

'Captain Benwick, would it not be better for Captain Benwick? He knows where a surgeon is to be found.'

Every one capable of thinking felt the advantage of the idea, and in a moment (it was all done in rapid moments) Captain Benwick had resigned the poor corpse-like figure entirely to the brother's care, and was off for the town with the utmost rapidity.

As to the wretched party left behind, it could scarcely be said which of the three, who were completely rational, was suffering most, Captain Wentworth, Anne, or Charles, who, really a very affectionate brother, hung over Louisa with sobs of grief, and could only turn his eyes from one sister, to see the other in a state as insensible, or to witness the hysterical agitations of his wife, calling on him for health which he could not give.

Anne, attending with all the strength and zeal, and thought, which instinct supplied, to Henrietta, still tried, at intervals, to suggest comfort to the others, tried to quiet Mary, to animate Charles, to assuage the feelings of Captain Wentworth. Both seemed to look to her for directions.

'Anne, Anne,' cried Charles, 'what is to be done next? What, in heaven's name, is to be done next?

Captain Wentworth's eyes were also turned towards her. 'Had not she be better carried to the inn? Yes, I am sure, carry her gently to the inn.'

'Yes, yes, to the inn,' repeated Captain Wentworth, comparatively collected, and eager to be doing something. 'I will carry her myself. Musgrove, take care of the others.'

By this time the report of the accident had spread among the workmen and boatmen about the Cobb, and many were collected near them, to be useful if wanted, at any rate, to enjoy the sight of a dead young lady, nay, two dead young ladies, for it proved twice as fine as the first report. To some of the best-looking of these good people Henrietta was consigned, for, though partially revived, she was quite helpless; and in this manner, Anne walking by her side, and Charles attending to his wife, they set forward, treading back with feelings unutterable, the ground which so lately, so very lately, and so light of heart, they had passed along.

They were not off the Cobb, before the Harvilles met them. Captain Benwick had been seen flying by their house, with a countenance which shewed something to be wrong; and they had set off immediately, informed and directed, as they passed, towards the spot. Shocked as Captain Harville was, he brought senses and nerves that could be instantly useful; and a look between him and his wife decided what was to be done. She must be taken to their house—all must go to their house—and wait the surgeon's arrival there. They would not listen to scruples; he was obeyed; they were all beneath his roof; and while Louisa, under Mrs Harville's direction, was conveyed up stairs, and given possession of her own bed, assistance, cordials, restoratives were supplied by her husband to all who needed them.

Louisa had once opened her eyes, but soon closed them again, without apparent consciousness. This had been a proof of life, however, of service to her sister; and Henrietta, though perfectly incapable of being in the same room with Louisa, was kept, by the agitation of hope and fear, from a return of her own insensibility. Mary, too, was growing calmer.

The surgeon was with them almost before it had seemed possible. They were sick with horror while he examined; but he was not hopeless. The head had received a severe contusion, but he had seen greater injuries recovered from; he was by no means hopeless; he spoke cheerfully.

That he did not regard it as a desperate case—that he did not say a few hours must end it—was at first felt, beyond the hope of most; and the ecstasy of such a reprieve, the rejoicing, deep and silent, after a few fervent ejaculations of gratitude to Heaven had been offered, may be conceived.

The tone, the look, with which 'Thank God!' was uttered by Captain Wentworth, Anne was sure could never be forgotten by her; nor the sight of him afterwards, as he sat near a table, leaning over it with folded arms, and face concealed, as if overpowered by the various feelings of his soul, and trying by prayer and reflection to calm them.

Louisa's limbs had escaped. There was no injury but to the head.

[Louisa duly recovers; in the end she accepts Captain Benwick. Anne and Wentworth are reunited.]

JOHN FOWLES

On the Undercliff

John Fowles, who lives in Lyme Regis, is much admired for such novels as *The Collector* (1963), *The Magus* (1966), and *The French Lieutenant's Woman* (1969) from which we print the Undercliff scene; the book has recently been filmed.

And once, but once, she lifted her eyes,
And suddenly, sweetly, strangely blush'd
To find they were met by my own. . .
                    TENNYSON, *Maud* (1855)

. . . with its green chasms between romantic rocks, where the scattered forest trees and orchards of luxuriant growth declare that many a generation must have passed away since the first partial falling of the cliff prepared the ground for such a state, where a scene so wonderful and so lovely is exhibited, as may more than equal any of the resembling scenes of the far-famed Isle of Wight. . .
                    JANE AUSTEN, *Persuasion*

There runs, between Lyme Regis and Axmouth six miles to the west, one of the strangest coastal landscapes in Southern England. From the air it is not very striking; one notes merely that whereas elsewhere on the coast the fields run to the cliff edge, here they stop

a mile or so short of it. The cultivated chequer of green and
red-brown breaks, with a kind of joyous indiscipline, into a dark
cascade of trees and undergrowth. There are no roofs. If one flies
low enough one can see that the terrain is very abrupt, cut by deep
chasms and accented by strange bluffs and towers of chalk and flint,
which loom over the lush foliage around them like the walls of
ruined castles. From the air . . . but on foot this seemingly un-
important wilderness gains a strange extension. People have been
lost in it for hours, and cannot believe, when they see on the map
where they were lost, that their sense of isolation—and if the
weather be bad, desolation—could have seemed so great.

The Undercliff—for this land is really the mile-long slope caused
by the erosion of the ancient vertical cliff-face—is very steep. Flat
places are as rare as visitors in it. But this steepness in effect tilts it,
and its vegetation, towards the sun; and it is this fact, together with
the water from the countless springs that have caused the erosion,
that lends the area its botanical strangeness—its wild arbutus and
ilex and other trees rarely seen growing in England; its enormous
ashes and beeches; its green Brazilian chasms choked with ivy and
the liana of wild clematis; its bracken that grows seven, eight feet
tall; its flowers that bloom a month earlier than anywhere else in
the district. In summer it is the nearest this country can offer to a
tropical jungle. It has also, like all land that has never been worked
or lived on by man, its mysteries, its shadows, its dangers—only too
literal ones geologically, since there are crevices and sudden falls
that can bring disaster, and in places where a man with a broken leg
could shout all week and not be heard. Strange as it may seem, it
was slightly less solitary a hundred years ago than it is today. There
is not a single cottage in the Undercliff now; in 1867 there were
several, lived in by gamekeepers, woodmen, a pigherd or two. The
roedeer, sure proof of abundant solitude, then must have passed
less peaceful days. Now the Undercliff has reverted to a state of
total wildness. The cottage walls have crumbled into ivied stumps,
the old branch paths have gone; no car road goes near it, the one
remaining track that traverses it is often impassable. And it is so by
Act of Parliament: a national nature reserve. Not all is lost to
expedience.

It was this place, an English Garden of Eden on such a day as
March 29th, 1867, that Charles had entered when he had climbed

the path from the shore at Pinhay Bay; and it was this same place whose eastern half was called Ware Commons.

When Charles had quenched his thirst and cooled his brow with his wetted handkerchief he began to look seriously around him. Or at least he tried to look seriously around him: but the little slope on which he found himself, the prospect before him, the sounds, the scents, the unalloyed wildness of growth and burgeoning fertility, forced him into anti-science. The ground about him was studded gold and pale yellow with celandines and primroses and banked by the bridal white of densely blossoming sloe; where jubilantly green-tipped elders shaded the mossy banks of the little brook he had drunk from were clusters of moschatel and woodsorrel, most delicate of English spring flowers. Higher up the slope he saw the white heads of anemones, and beyond them deep green drifts of bluebell leaves. A distant woodpecker drummed in the branches of some high tree, and bullfinches whistled quietly over his head; newly arrived chiffchaffs and willow-warblers sang in every bush and treetop. When he turned he saw the blue sea, now washing far below; and the whole extent of Lyme Bay reaching round, diminishing cliffs that dropped into the endless yellow sabre of the Chesil Bank, whose remote tip touched that strange English Gibraltar, Portland Bill, a thin grey shadow wedged between azures.

Only one art has ever caught such scenes—that of the Renaissance; it is the ground that Botticelli's figures walk on, the air that includes Ronsard's songs. It does not matter what that cultural revolution's conscious aims and purposes, its cruelties and failures were; in essence the Renaissance was simply the green end of one of civilisation's hardest winters. It was an end to chains, bounds, frontiers. Its device was the only device: What is, is good. It was all, in short, that Charles's age was not; but do not think that as he stood there he did not know this. It is true that to explain his obscure feeling of malaise, of inappropriateness, of limitation, he went back closer home—to Rousseau, and the childish myths of a Golden Age and the Noble Savage. That is, he tried to dismiss the inadequacies of his own time's approach to nature by supposing that one cannot re-enter a legend. He told himself he was too pampered, too spoilt by civilisation, ever to inhabit nature again;

and that made him sad, in a not unpleasant bitter-sweet sort of way. After all, he was a Victorian. We could not expect him to see what we are only just beginning—and with so much more knowledge and the lessons of existentialist philosophy at our disposal—to realise ourselves: that the desire to hold and the desire to enjoy are mutually destructive. His statement to himself should have been, 'I possess this now, therefore I am happy', instead of what it so Victorianly was: 'I cannot possess this for ever, and therefore am sad.'

Science eventually regained its hegemony, and he began to search among the beds of flint along the course of the stream for his tests. He found a pretty fragment of fossil scallop, but the sea-urchins eluded him. Gradually he moved through the trees to the west, bending, carefully quartering the ground with his eyes; moving on a few paces, then repeating the same procedure. Now and then he would turn over a likely-looking flint with the end of his ashplant. But he had no luck. An hour passed, and his duty towards Ernestina began to outweigh his lust for echinoderms. He looked at his watch, repressed a curse, and made his way back to where he had left his rucksack. Some way up the slope, with the declining sun on his back, he came on a path and set off for Lyme. The path climbed and curved slightly inward beside an ivy-grown stone wall and then—in the unkind manner of paths—forked without indication. He hesitated, then walked some fifty yards or so along the lower path, which lay sunk in a transverse gulley, already deeply shadowed. But then he came to a solution to his problem—not knowing exactly how the land lay—for yet another path suddenly branched to his right, back towards the sea, up a steep small slope crowned with grass, and from which he could plainly orientate himself. He therefore pushed up through the strands of bramble—the path was seldom used—to the little green plateau.

It opened out very agreeably, like a tiny alpine meadow. The white scuts of three or four rabbits explained why the turf was so short.

Charles stood in the sunlight. Eyebright and birdsfoot starred the grass, and already vivid green clumps of marjoram reached up to bloom. Then he moved forward to the edge of the plateau.

And there, below him, he saw a figure.

For one terrible moment he thought he had stumbled on a corpse. But it was a woman asleep. She had chosen the strangest position, a broad, sloping ledge of grass some five feet beneath the level of the plateau, and which hid her from the view of any but one who came, as Charles had, to the very edge. The chalk walls behind this little natural balcony made it into a sun-trap, for its widest axis pointed south-west. But it was not a sun-trap many would have chosen. Its outer edge gave on to a sheer drop of some thirty or forty feet into an ugly tangle of brambles. A little beyond them the real cliff plunged down to the beach.

Charles's immediate instinct had been to draw back out of the woman's view. He did not see who she was. He stood at a loss, looking at but not seeing the fine landscape the place commanded. He hesitated, he was about to withdraw; but then his curiosity drew him forward again.

The girl lay in the complete abandonment of deep sleep, on her back. Her coat had fallen open over her indigo dress, unrelieved in its calico severity except by a small white collar at the throat. The sleeper's face was turned away from him, her right arm thrown back, bent in a childlike way. A scattered handful of anemones lay on the grass around it. There was something intensely tender and yet sexual in the way she lay; it awakened a dim echo in Charles of a moment from his time in Paris. Another girl, whose name now he could not even remember, perhaps had never known, seen sleeping so, one dawn, in a bedroom overlooking the Seine.

He moved round the curving lip of the plateau, to where he could see the sleeper's face better, and it was only then that he realised whom he had intruded upon. It was the French Lieutenant's Woman. Part of her hair had become loose and half-covered her cheek. On the Cobb it had seemed to him a dark brown; now he saw that it had red tints, a rich warmth, and without the then indispensable gloss of feminine hair-oil. The skin below seemed very brown, almost ruddy, in that light, as if the girl cared more for health than a fashionably pale and languid-cheeked complexion. A strong nose, heavy eyebrows . . . the mouth he could not see. It irked him strangely that he had to see her upside down, since the land would not allow him to pass round for the proper angle.

He stood unable to do anything but stare down, tranced by this unexpected encounter, and overcome by an equally strange feeling —not sexual, but fraternal, perhaps paternal, a certainty of the innocence of this creature, of her being unfairly outcast, and which was in turn a factor of his intuition of her appalling loneliness. He could not imagine what, besides despair, could drive her, in an age where women were semi-static, timid, incapable of sustained physical effort, to this wild place.

He came at last to the very edge of the rampart above her, directly over her face, and there he saw that all the sadness he had so remarked before was gone; in sleep the face was gentle, it might even have had the ghost of a smile. It was precisely then, as he craned sideways down, that she awoke.

She looked up at once, so quickly that his step back was in vain. He was detected, and he was too much a gentleman to deny it. So when Sarah scrambled to her feet, gathering her coat about her, and stared back up at him from her ledge, he raised his wideawake and bowed. She said nothing, but fixed him with a look of shock and bewilderment, perhaps not untinged with shame. She had fine eyes, dark eyes.

They stood thus for several seconds, locked in a mutual incomprehension. She seemed so small to him, standing there below him, hidden from the waist down, clutching her collar, as if, should he take a step towards her, she would turn and fling herself out of his sight. He came to his sense of what was proper.

'A thousand apologies. I came upon you inadvertently.' And then he turned and walked away. He did not look back, but scrambled down to the path he had left, and back to the fork, where he wondered why he had not had the presence of mind to ask which path he was to take, and waited half a minute to see if she was following him. She did not appear. Very soon he marched firmly away up the steeper path.

Charles did not know it, but in those brief poised seconds above the waiting sea, in that luminous evening silence broken only by the waves' quiet wash, the whole Victorian Age was lost. And I do not mean he had taken the wrong path.

WINSTON GRAHAM

Jud's Funeral

This is a chapter from *Jeremy Poldark* (1950), one of the sequence of novels by Winston Graham, whose closely imagined Cornish life has also been familiar on television worldwide.

Jud Paynter's send-off fitty ways began at two o'clock the day before the funeral. Prudie had submerged her grief in the preparations, and a long table made of old boxes had been fastened together in the larger of the two rooms. More old boxes outside served as chairs and tables for those who couldn't squeeze in. And there were many such until the heavy rain of nightfall drove them away.

Prudie as chief mourner had managed to gather together enough black clothes to make an impressive display. Her cousin had lent her black stockings, and she'd made a skirt out of a piece of serge bought at Aunt Mary Rogers's shop. An old black blouse of her own was decorated with mourning beads and a bit of ragged lace, and Char Nanfan had actually produced a black veil. Barely recognisable in this array, she sat in a place of honour at the head of the table unmoving throughout the meal and waited on by Cousin Tina, Char Nanfan, Mrs Zacky Martin and a few of the younger end.

The Rev Mr Odgers had been invited to the feast but had discreetly declined; so pride of place next to the bereaved widow was given to Paul Daniel, who was Jud Paynter's oldest friend. On the other side was Constable Vage, who was conducting the inquiry into the murder, and others present were Zacky Martin, Charlie Kempthorne, Whitehead and Jinny Scoble, Ned Bottrell, Uncle Ben and Aunt Sarah Tregeagle, Jack Cobbledick, the Curnow brothers, Aunt Betsy Triggs, and some fifteen or twenty assorted hangers-on.

Soon after two the feast began with a long draught of raw brandy all round, and then everyone set to eating and drinking at a great rate as if there wasn't a minute to be lost. At the outset the splendid widow ate more genteelly than the rest, taking in nourishment under the heavy veil as under a visor. But as the brandy warmed her vitals she threw back the emblem of bereavement and tucked in with the rest.

About five the first part of the feast was over, and by sunset many of the women began to drift off, having families or homes to see to, and the number in the room came down to about a score. This was twice as many as could decently breathe in a cramped space already full of smoke and steam and tobacco fumes. Jugs of brandy, rum and gin were now going round freely, with hot water and sugar to be added to taste. At this point the hymns began. Uncle Ben Tregeagle, as doyen of the church choir, was allowed to lead them, and Joe Permewan scraped an accompaniment like rusty metal on his bass viol. They sang all the hymns and anthems they knew and some they didn't know, and then got on to patriotic songs. They sang 'God Save the King' four times . . . and a few ditties that weren't too savoury if looked at in the most formal light.

But now no one was feeling formal, least of all Prudie, who, her nose shining like a hurricane lamp, allowed herself to be persuaded to get up and sing a song which had the chorus:

> An' when he died, he shut his eyes,
> An' never saw money no more.

Then Aunt Betsy Triggs got up and did her famous dance, ending up sitting in Constable Vage's lap. The roar that greeted this dwindled to a shamefaced silence as everyone came to realise they were overstepping the traces.

Prudie worked her feet into her tattered carpet slippers and slowly got up again.

'My dear, *dear* friends,' she said, 'don't take on on account o' me, I beg you. Take no heed of my grief. An' take no heed of the ole man out there that's going to be teeled tomorrer. Tis just a per-personal matter twixt 'im and me. No reason why ye have got to stay quiet as meaders just on account o' that. Eat, drink an' do what you will, for tis no affair of his what I do with his money now 'e's going to his long lie.' She hunched her great shoulders and glowered. 'I-facks, tis more'n I can b'lieve 'ow he did conceal the gold away from me all these many year. Hid it from his own wife, 'e did. Or as near his wife as makes no concern.'

Charlie Kempthorne tittered, but Constable Vage poked him solemnly in the ribs and shook his head; that was not the place to show amusement.

'My blessed life,' said Prudie, and hiccupped. 'He was a whited sepulchre, was my old man, if the truth be known. An' old cloamin tomcat hollow to the toes. As cuzzle as they come. I'd as lief trust a beaver. But there twas, that's how tis, an' no one can deny it. 'E was my old man, see.'

Paul Daniel grunted. After the merriment everyone was feeling sentimental and full of liquor.

'An' he was a talker when the drink was in him. Talk. 'E'd outtalk preacher any day of the week, Sundays including. But I seen him goin' down'ill for months. Twasn't all murdering lyin' thiefs what done for him. Twas semi-decay. Tha's what twas. He'd lived a hard life an' it told in the end.'

She sat down abruptly before she had finished because her knees gave way. Constable Vage got up. At ordinary times he was a wheelwright.

'Brothers and sisters,' he said. 'I aren't one for slack-jaw as ye all well know; but it wouldn't do if we ended this feastin' without a thought or two for our dear brother Jud, newly departed to the flowery fields and green meads o' paradise. Wicked men 'as struck him down, but the law will track them out, never doubt.' He folded his hands over his stomach.

' 'Ear, 'ear,' said Prudie.

'So we must not forget the vacant chair at this table.' Vage looked round but could not see even an empty packing case.

'The vacant chair,' he repeated. 'And it is only right an' proper that we drink a toast to our dear departed brother.'

'A-a-is,' said Tina.

'To our dear brother,' said Prudie, raising her glass.

The toast was drunk.

'May he rest easy,' said Joe Permewan.

'Amen,' said Uncle Ben Tregeagle, shaking his ringlets.

'Tis a poor life,' said Aunt Sarah. 'From the cradle to the grave in two snaps of the fingers. I see it all. Layin' out and lyin' in. That's me job, but it makes you think.'

'Amen,' said Uncle Ben.

'I'd sooner be a fish jouster any day,' said Betsy.

'There's many I've found worser to lay out than Jud,' said Sarah. ' 'E stretched out a good deal of a long man, but there warn't so much round the middle as I suspected.'

'Amen,' said Uncle Ben.

' 'Old hard with your "amens", old man,' said Prudie. 'We aren't in church yet. You can say yer prayers tomorrow.'

Charlie Kempthorne began to giggle. He giggled and giggled until everyone hushed him for fear he'd wake the guests already asleep on the floor.

'I aren't partic'lar what I do for the living,' said Betsy. 'But when they ain't living they give me the shrims. Even poor Joe I didn' dare touch—an' him me own brother these fifty year or more.' She began to weep gently.

' 'Ere, Ned,' said Prudie, 'do ee go'n draw the spigot of that next keg of brandy. I'm as thirsty as a cat wi' nine chets. Tis early yet.'

Bottrell winked at her and went into the other room, which had served as a kitchen today. Prudie sat back, her massive arms folded, surveying the scene with a satisfied expression. Everything had gone off handsome so far. Most of the remaining guests would sleep here the night, and tomorrow, pleasurable thought, it would all begin again. The burying was at noon, so they'd have the coffin out early if it was fine, and placed outside the door on a bench of chairs and packing cases. All the other mourners would be back straight after breakfast, and they'd begin singing hymns. One hymn and then a glass, another hymn and then another glass until about eleven o'clock. Then the bearers would take up the coffin and carry it a hundred yards or so, and Ned Bottrell would follow behind with an anker of brandy and they'd have a hymn and refreshments, another hundred yards and more refreshments, until they got to the church. They should manage that by twelve o'clock, if they managed it at all. Prudie remembered that real bumper funeral of Tommy Job's when the bearers had been stretched out flat with still a mile to go.

Aunt Sarah Tregeagle said: 'When I first started layin' out, mind, it used to shrim me up too, so I did used to say a little charm over to meself that I'd learned from Grannie Nanpusker, that was a white witch. Afore ever I laid me 'ands on one that'd gone dead I used to say: "God save us from mystifications, conjurations, toxifications, incantations, fumigations, tarnations, devilations and damnations. Amen. Rosemary, tansy, sweet briar, herb o' grace." An' I never come to no 'arm at all.'

'My blessed Parliament,' said Prudie.

'Amen,' echoed Uncle Ben sleepily.

But there was nothing sleepy in the way Ned Bottrell burst back into the room. He wasn't carrying any brandy, and his face was white.

'It's gone!' he shouted.

'The brandy!' said Prudie, lurching to her feet. ' 'Ere, who's stolen it? Twas there an hour gone—'

'Not all *three* kegs!' said Constable Vage, instantly alert. 'Why we did oughter have heard them. They couldn't move three kegs without—'

'Nay,' said Ned Bottrell, shouting above the clamour. 'Not the drink, the corpse!'

They got it out of him bit by bit, in a rising clamour of voices. Lured by morbid curiosity and professional pride, he had carried the lantern from the kitchen and taken a peep in the shed, just, as he put it, to see if the ole man was comfortable in his nice new box. And there was the coffin, but the body was gone.

Some of them were as shaken as Ned, but Prudie took the situation firmly in hand. First she said Ned was as full as a can and couldn't see straight and the ole man was still there, she'd lay a guinea. But when Ned invited her to come and see, she said her feet was hurting her and sent Constable Vage instead.

When Vage, clearing his throat a good deal and patting his stomach, returned to confirm the story, she drained another glass and stood up.

'Tis they body stealers,' she said in a booming voice. 'You d'now what tis like. I reckon tis those same thievin' lyin' murderers that corpsed him on Monday night. Come us on, my sons.'

With a great show of resolution a dozen of them, led now by the widow, pushed through into the lean-to shed and stared down at Ned Bottrell's box. It looked a good bit of carpentry, and even in this moment of crisis Ned couldn't refrain from giving it an admiring glance. But it was quite empty.

Prudie nearly tipped it up by sitting suddenly on the edge and bursting into tears.

'There, there, now,' said Paul Daniel, who had been wakened from a sound sleep and dragged in here without a full explanation. 'It edn as if he'd been took sudden. We was all prepared for the worst.'

'He's been took sudden, sure 'nough,' said Joe Permewan. 'Tis *where* 'e's been took that's mystifying me.'

'We can't 'ave a funeral without someone to teel,' said Betsy Triggs. 'Twouldn't be decent.'

'There, there, now,' said Paul Daniel, stroking Prudie's lank hair. 'You must be brave, my dear. We've all got to come to it sooner or later. Rich an' poor, gentle an' simple, saint an' sinner. We all must be brave.'

'Brave be *danged!*' shouted Prudie, reacting ungratefully. 'Go hold yer 'ead! I want to know what they done wi' my ole man!'

There was a brief silence.

'We must look,' said Constable Vage. 'Maybe he hasn't been took far.'

This suggestion seemed better than doing nothing, so two more lanterns were lit. When they opened the door it was raining heavily and was pitch-dark, but after some shufflings and hesitation three small search parties were organised, while the women went back to the feast to console Prudie.

Prudie was inconsolable. It was the disgrace, she said. To have a husband an' then not to have a husband, that was how she saw it, and she said she'd never live it down. Betsy Triggs was quite right, you couldn't have a burying without someone to bury. The lying murdering thieves had not only robbed her of her old man, they'd even taken away the pleasure of seeing him planted decent. Everyone was coming back tomorrow for a proper slap-up funeral, and there was three ankers of brandy not touched yet, and all those pies and cakes, and the preacher engaged, and the hole dug, and nothing to put in it. It was more than flesh and blood could stand.

Aunt Sarah Tregeagle thought she'd help the time away with a story of one of her layings out, when a man had died with his knees up; but no one seemed to want to listen, so in the end she tailed off and silence fell. This was nearly as bad, they found, so Uncle Ben, who had been excused the search on account of age, turned to Joe Permewan, who had been excused the search on account of rheumatics, and asked him to play a tune. Joe said, all right, it was just what he'd thought of suggesting himself, and got out his bass viol; but he was so fuddled with drink that when he came to play, the noise he made was even worse than the silence. As Prudie said, it was just as if he was drawing the bow over his own guts.

Ben then suggested a singsong, but nobody had the breath for this, and Prudie began to take offence at Jack Cobbledick's snores from the corner under the window. It was insult on insult, she said. However, no amount of thumping would wake him, so they just went on and on.

Then Betsy Triggs heard footsteps at the door and they all waited eagerly to see what news the returning searchers brought.

Jud Paynter limped in. He was in his best underclothes and was very wet and very cross. The tablecloth he'd borrowed from the kiddley down the lane wasn't much protection from the rain.

' 'Ere,' he said truculently, 'what's all this? An' where's my pipe?'

'Q'

The Roll-Call of the Reef

The late Sir Arthur Quiller-Couch ('Q'), 1863-1944, nonpareil of Cornish writers, included this famous story in his collection, *Wandering Heath* (1895). He was then at Fowey—the 'Troy' of his books—where, since 1892, he had made what would be a permanent home at The Haven. The scene of 'The Roll-Call of the Reef' is the east coast of the Lizard peninsula. Deadliest of reefs, the Manacles are half-tide rocks that have claimed many wrecks; hundreds of victims are buried in St Keverne churchyard.

'Yes, sir,' said my host the quarryman, reaching down the relics from their hook in the wall over the chimney-piece; 'they've hung there all my time, and most of my father's. The women won't touch 'em; they're afraid of the story. So here they'll dangle, and gather dust and smoke, till another tenant comes and tosses 'em out o' doors for rubbish. Whew! 'tis coarse weather.'

He went to the door, opened it, and stood studying the gale that beat upon his cottage-front, straight from the Manacle Reef. The rain drove past him into the kitchen, aslant like threads of gold silk in the shine of the wreckwood fire. Meanwhile by the same firelight I examined the relics on my knee. The metal of each was tarnished out of knowledge. But the trumpet was evidently an old cavalry trumpet, and the threads of its parti-coloured sling, though frayed and dusty, still hung together. Around the side-drum, beneath its cracked brown varnish, I could hardly trace a royal coat-of-arms, and a legend running— *Per Mare per Terram*—the motto of the Marines. Its parchment, though coloured and scented with wood-smoke, was limp and mildewed; and I began to tighten up the straps—under which the drumsticks had been loosely thrust—with the idle purpose of trying if some music might be got out of the old drum yet.

But as I turned it on my knee, I found the drum attached to the trumpet-sling by a curious barrel-shaped padlock, and paused to examine this. The body of the lock was composed of half a dozen brass rings, set accurately edge to edge; and, rubbing the brass with my thumb, I saw that each of the six had a series of letters engraved around it.

I knew the trick of it, I thought. Here was one of those word-padlocks, once so common; only to be opened by getting the rings to spell a certain word, which the dealer confides to you.

My host shut and barred the door, and came back to the hearth.

' 'Twas just such a wind—east by south—that brought in what you've got between your hands. Back in the year 'nine it was; my father has told me the tale a score o' times. You're twisting round the rings, I see. But you'll never guess the word. Parson Kendall, he made the word, and locked down a couple o' ghosts in their graves with it; and when his time came, he went to his own grave and took the word with him.'

'Whose ghosts, Matthew?'

'You want the story, I see, sir. My father could tell it better than I can. He was a young man in the year 'nine, unmarried at the time, and living in this very cottage just as I be. That's how he came to get mixed up with the tale.'

He took a chair, lit a short pipe, and unfolded the story in a low musing voice, with his eyes fixed on the dancing violet flames.

'Yes, he'd ha' been about thirty year old in January, of the year 'nine. The storm got up in the night o' the twenty-first o' that month. My father was dressed and out long before daylight; he never was one to 'bide in bed, let be that the gale by this time was pretty near lifting the thatch over his head. Besides which, he'd fenced a small 'taty-patch that winter, down by Lowland Point, and he wanted to see if it stood the night's work. He took the path across Gunner's Meadow—where they buried most of the bodies afterwards. The wind was right in his teeth at the time, and once on the way (he's told me this often) a great strip of oreweed came flying through the darkness and fetched him a slap on the cheek like a cold hand. But he made shift pretty well till he got to Lowland, and then had to drop upon his hands and knees and crawl, digging his fingers every now and then into the shingle to hold on, for he declared to me that the stones, some of them as big as a man's head, kept rolling and driving past till it seemed the whole foreshore was moving westward under him. The fence was gone, of course; not a stick left to show where it stood; so that, when first he came to the place, he thought he must have missed his bearings. My father, sir, was a very religious man; and if he reckoned the end of the world was at hand—there in the great wind and night, among the moving stones—you may believe he was certain of it when he heard a gun fired, and, with the same, saw a flame shoot up out of the darkness to windward, making a sudden fierce light in all the place about. All he could find to think or say was, "The Second Coming—The Second Coming! The Bridegroom cometh, and the wicked He will toss like a ball into a large country!" and being already upon his knees, he just bowed his head and 'bided, saying this over and over.

'But by'm-by, between two squalls, he made bold to lift his head and look, and then by the light—a bluish colour 'twas—he saw all the coast clear away to Manacle Point, and off the Manacles, in the thick of the weather, a sloop-of-war with top-gallants housed, driving stern foremost towards the reef. It was she, of course, that was burning the flare. My father could see the white streak and the ports of her quite plain as she rose to it, a little outside the breakers, and he guessed easy enough that her captain had just managed to wear ship, and was trying to force her nose to the sea with the help of her small bower anchor and the scrap or two of canvas that hadn't yet been blown out of her. But while he looked, she fell off, giving her broadside to it foot by foot, and drifting back on the breakers around Carn dû and the Varses. The rocks lie so thick thereabouts, that 'twas a toss up which she struck first; at any rate, my father couldn't tell at the time, for just then the flare died down and went out.

'Well, sir, he turned then in the dark and started back for Coverack to cry the dismal tidings—though well knowing ship and crew to be past any hope; and as he turned, the wind lifted him and tossed him forward "like a ball", as he'd been saying, and homeward along the foreshore. As you know, 'tis ugly work, even by daylight, picking your way among the stones there, and my father was prettily knocked about at first in the dark. But by this 'twas nearer seven than six o'clock, and the day spreading. By the time he reached North Corner, a man could see to read print; hows'ever, he looked neither out to sea nor towards Coverack, but headed straight for the first cottage—the same that stands above North Corner today. A man named Billy Ede lived there then, and when my father burst into the kitchen bawling, "Wreck! wreck!" he saw Billy Ede's wife, Ann, standing there in her clogs, with a shawl over her head, and her clothes wringing wet.

' "Save the chap!" says Billy Ede's wife, Ann. "What d' 'ee mean by crying stale fish at that rate?"

' "But 'tis a wreck, I tell 'ee. I've a-zeed 'n!"

' "Why, so 'tis," says she, "and I've a-zeed 'n too; and so has everyone with an eye in his head."

'And with that she pointed straight over my father's shoulder, and he turned; and there, close under Dolor Point, at the end of Coverack town, he saw *another* wreck washing, and the point black with people, like emmets, running to and fro in the morning light. While he stood staring at her, he heard a trumpet sounded on board, the notes coming in little jerks, like a bird rising against the wind; but faintly, of course, because of the distance and the gale blowing—though this had dropped a little.

' "She's a transport," said Billy Ede's wife, Ann, "and full of horse soldiers, fine long men. When she struck they must ha' pitched the hosses over first to lighten the ship, for a score of dead hosses had washed in afore I left, half an hour back. An' three or four soldiers, too—fine long corpses in white breeches and jackets of blue and gold. I held the lantern to one. Such a straight young man!"

'My father asked her about the trumpeting.

' "That's the queerest bit of all. She was burnin' a light when

me an' my man joined the crowd down there. All her masts had
gone; whether they carried away, or were cut away to ease her,
I don't rightly know. Anyway, there she lay 'pon the rocks with
her decks bare. Her keelson was broke under her and her bottom
sagged and stove, and she had just settled down like a sitting hen—
just the leastest list to starboard; but a man could stand there easy.
They had rigged up ropes across her, from bulwark to bulwark,
an' beside these the men were mustered, holding on like grim
death whenever the sea made a clean breach over them, an'
standing up like heroes as soon as it passed. The captain an' the
officers were clinging to the rail of the quarter-deck, all in their
golden uniforms, waiting for the end as if 'twas King George
they expected. There was no way to help, for she lay right beyond
cast of line, though our folk tried it fifty times. And beside them
clung a trumpeter, a whacking big man, an' between the heavy
seas he would lift his trumpet with one hand, and blow a call;
and every time he blew, the men gave a cheer. There" (she says)
"—hark 'ee now—there he goes agen! But you won't hear no
cheering any more, for few are left to cheer, and their voices weak.
Bitter cold the wind is, and I reckon it numbs their grip o' the
ropes, for they were dropping off fast with every sea when my
man sent me home to get his breakfast. *Another* wreck, you say?
Well, there's no hope for the tender dears, if 'tis the Manacles.
You'd better run down and help yonder; though 'tis little help
that any man can give. Not one came in alive while I was there.
The tide's flowing, an' she won't hold together another hour,
they say."

'Well, sure enough, the end was coming fast when my father
got down to the point. Six men had been cast up alive, or just
breathing—a seaman and five troopers. The seaman was the only
one that had breath to speak; and while they were carrying him
into the town, the word went round that the ship's name was the
Despatch, transport, homeward bound from Corunna, with a
detachment of the 7th Hussars, that had been fighting out there
with Sir John Moore. The seas had rolled her farther over by this
time, and given her decks a pretty sharp slope; but a dozen men
still held on, seven by the ropes near the ship's waist, a couple
near the break of the poop, and three on the quarter-deck. Of
these three my father made out one to be the skipper; close by

him clung an officer in full regimentals—his name, they heard after, was Captain Duncanfield; and last came the tall trumpeter; and if you'll believe me, the fellow was making shift there, at the very last, to blow "God Save the King". What's more, he got to "Send us victorious" before an extra big sea came bursting across and washed them off the deck—every man but one of the pair beneath the poop—and *he* dropped his hold before the next wave; being stunned, I reckon. The others went out of sight at once, but the trumpeter—being, as I said, a powerful man as well as a tough swimmer—rose like a duck, rode out a couple of breakers, and came in on the crest of the third. The folks looked to see him broke like an egg at their feet; but when the smother cleared, there he was, lying face downward on a ledge below them; and one of the men that happened to have a rope round him—I forget the fellow's name, if I ever heard it—jumped down and grabbed him by the ankle as he began to slip back. Before the next big sea, the pair were hauled high enough to be out of harm, and another heave brought them up to grass. Quick work; but master trumpeter wasn't quite dead; nothing worse than a cracked head and three staved ribs. In twenty minutes or so they had him in bed, with the doctor to tend him.

'Now was the time—nothing being left alive upon the transport— for my father to tell of the sloop he'd seen driving upon the Manacles. And when he got a hearing, though the most were set upon salvage, and believed a wreck in the hand, so to say, to be worth half a dozen they couldn't see, a good few volunteered to start off with him and have a look. They crossed Lowland Point; no ship to be seen on the Manacles, nor anywhere upon the sea. One or two was for calling my father a liar. "Wait till we come to Dean Point," said he. Sure enough, on the far side of Dean Point, they found the sloop's mainmast washing about with half a dozen men lashed to it—men in red jackets—every mother's son drowned and staring; and a little farther on, just under the Dean, three or four bodies cast up on the shore, one of them a small drummer-boy, side-drum and all; and, near by, part of a ship's gig, with "HMS *Primrose*" cut on the stern-board. From this point on, the shore was littered thick with wreckage and dead bodies— the most of them Marines in uniform; and in Godrevy Cove, in particular, a heap of furniture from the captain's cabin, and amongst it a water-tight box, not much damaged, and full of papers; by which, when it came to be examined next day, the wreck was easily made out to be the *Primrose*, of eighteen guns, outward bound from Portsmouth, with a fleet of transports for the Spanish War—thirty sail, I've heard, but I've never heard what became of them. Being handled by merchant skippers, no doubt they rode out the gale and reached the Tagus safe and sound. Not but what the captain of the *Primrose* (Mein was his name) did quite right to try and club-haul his vessel when he found himself under the land: only he never ought to have got there if he took proper soundings. But it's easy talking.

'The *Primrose*, sir, was a handsome vessel—for her size, one of the handsomest in the King's service—and newly fitted out at Plymouth Dock. So the boys had brave pickings from her in the way of brass-work, ship's instruments, and the like, let alone some barrels of stores not much spoiled. They loaded themselves with as much as they could carry, and started for home, meaning to make a second journey before the preventive men got wind of their doings and came to spoil the fun. But as my father was passing back under the Dean, he happened to take a look over his shoulder at the bodies there. "Hullo," says he, and dropped his gear: "I do believe there's a leg moving!" And, running fore, he stooped over the small drummer-boy that I told you about. The poor little chap was lying there, with his face a mass of bruises and his eyes closed: but he had shifted one leg an inch or two, and was still breathing. So my father pulled out a knife and cut him free from his drum—that was lashed on to him with a double turn of Manilla rope—and took him up and carried him along here, to this very room that we're sitting in. He lost a good deal by this, for when he went back to fetch his bundle the preventive men had got hold of it, and were thick as thieves along the fore-shore; so that 'twas only by paying one or two to look the other way that he picked up anything worth carrying off: which you'll allow to be hard, seeing that he was the first man to give news of the wreck.

'Well, the inquiry was held, of course, and my father gave evidence; and for the rest they had to trust to the sloop's papers: for not a soul was saved besides the drummer-boy, and he was raving in a fever, brought on by the cold and the fright. And the seamen and the five troopers gave evidence about the loss of the *Despatch*. The tall trumpeter, too, whose ribs were healing, came forward and kissed the Book; but somehow his head had been hurt in coming ashore, and he talked foolish-like, and 'twas easy seen he would never be a proper man again. The others were taken up to Plymouth, and so went their ways; but the trumpeter stayed on in Coverack; and King George, finding he was fit for nothing, sent him down a trifle of a pension after a while—enough to keep him in board and lodging, with a bit of tobacco over.

'Now the first time that this man—William Tallifer, he called himself—met with the drummer-boy, was about a fortnight after the little chap had bettered enough to be allowed a short walk out of doors, which he took, if you please, in full regimentals. There never was a soldier so proud of his dress. His own suit had shrunk a brave bit with the salt water; but into ordinary frock an' corduroys he declared he would not get—not if he had to go naked the rest of his life; so my father, being a good-natured man and handy with the needle, turned to and repaired damages with a piece or two of scarlet cloth cut from the jacket of one of the drowned Marines. Well, the poor little chap chanced to be standing, in this rig-out, down by the gate of Gunner's Meadow, where they had buried two score and over of his comrades. The morning was a fine one, early in March month; and along came the cracked trumpeter, likewise taking a stroll.

' "Hullo!" says he; "good mornin'! And what might you be doin' here?"

' "I was a-wishin'," says the boy, "I had a pair o' drum-sticks. Our lads were buried yonder without so much as a drum tapped or a musket fired; and that's not Christian burial for British soldiers."

' "Phut!" says the trumpeter, and spat on the ground; "a parcel of Marines!"

'The boy eyed him a second or so, and answered up: "If I'd a tab of turf handy, I'd bung it at your mouth, you greasy cavalry-man, and learn you to speak respectful of your betters. The Marines are the handiest body of men in the service."

'The trumpeter looked down on him from the height of six foot two, and asked: "Did they die well?"

' "They died very well. There was a lot of running to and fro
at first, and some of the men began to cry, and a few to strip off
their clothes. But when the ship fell off for the last time, Captain
Mein turned and said something to Major Griffiths, the commanding officer on board, and the Major called out to me to beat to
quarters. It might have been for a wedding, he sang it out so
cheerful. We'd had word already that 'twas to be parade order,
and the men fell in as trim and decent as if they were going to
church. One or two even tried to shave at the last moment. The
Major wore his medals. One of the seamen, seeing I had hard
work to keep the drum steady—the sling being a bit loose for me
and the wind what you remember—lashed it tight with a piece of
rope; and that saved my life afterwards, a drum being as good as
a cork until 'tis stove. I kept beating away until every man was on
deck; and then the Major formed them up and told them to die
like British soldiers, and the chaplain read a prayer or two—the
boys standin' all the while like rocks, each man's courage keeping
up the others'. The chaplain was in the middle of a prayer when
she struck. In ten minutes she was gone. That was how they died,
cavalryman."

' "And that was very well done, drummer of the Marines.
What's your name?"

' "John Christian."

' "Mine is William George Tallifer, trumpeter, of the 7th
Light Dragoons—the Queen's Own. I played 'God Save the
King' while our men were drowning. Captain Duncanfield told
me to sound a call or two, to put them in heart; but that matter
of 'God Save the King' was a notion of my own. I won't say
anything to hurt the feelings of a Marine, even if he's not much
over five-foot tall; but the Queen's Own Hussars is a tearin' fine
regiment. As between horse and foot, 'tis a question o' which
gets the chance. All the way from Sahagun to Corunna 'twas we
that took and gave the knocks—at Mayorga and Rueda, and
Bennyventy." (The reason, sir, I can speak the names so pat is
that my father learnt 'em by heart afterwards from the trumpeter,
who was always talking about Mayorga and Rueda and Bennyventy.) "We made the rear-guard, under General Paget, and
drove the French every time; and all the infantry did was to sit
about in wine-shops till we whipped 'em out, an' steal an' straggle

an' play the tom-fool in general. And when it came to a stand-up fight at Corunna, 'twas the horse, or the best part of it, that had to stay sea-sick aboard the transports, an' watch the infantry in the thick o' the caper. Very well they behaved, too; 'specially the 4th Regiment, an' the 42nd Highlanders an' the Dirty Half-Hundred. Oh, ay; they're decent regiments, all three. But the Queen's Own Hussars is a tearin' fine regiment. So you played on your drum when the ship was goin' down? Drummer John Christian, I'll have to get you a new pair o' drum-sticks for that."

'Well, sir, it appears that the very next day the trumpeter marched into Helston, and got a carpenter there to turn him a pair of box-wood drum-sticks for the boy. And this was the beginning of one of the most curious friendships you ever heard tell of. Nothing delighted the pair more than to borrow a boat off my father and pull out to the rocks where the *Primrose* and the *Despatch* had struck and sunk; and on still days 'twas pretty to hear them out there off the Manacles, the drummer playing his tattoo—for they always took their music with them—and the trumpeter practising calls, and making his trumpet speak like an angel. But if the weather turned roughish, they'd be walking together and talking; leastwise, the youngster listened while the other discoursed about Sir John's campaign in Spain and Portugal, telling how each little skirmish befell; and of Sir John himself, and General Baird and General Paget, and Colonel Vivian, his own commanding officer, and what kind of men they were; and of the last bloody stand-up at Corunna, and so forth, as if neither could have enough.

'But all this had to come to an end in the late summer; for the boy, John Christian, being now well and strong again, must go up to Plymouth to report himself. 'Twas his own wish (for I believe King George had forgotten all about him), but his friend wouldn't hold him back. As for the trumpeter, my father had made an arrangement to take him on as a lodger as soon as the boy left; and on the morning fixed for the start, he was up at the door here by five o'clock, with his trumpet slung by his side, and all the rest of his kit in a small valise. A Monday morning it was, and after breakfast he had fixed to walk with the boy some way on the road towards Helston, where the coach started. My father left them at breakfast together, and went out to meat the pig, and do a few odd morning jobs of that sort. When he came back, the boy was still at table, and the trumpeter standing here by the chimney-place with the drum and trumpet in his hands, hitched together just as they be at this moment.

‘ "Look at this," he says to my father, showing him the lock; "I picked it up off a starving brass-worker in Lisbon, and it is not one of your common locks that one word of six letters will open at any time. There's *janius* in this lock; for you've only to make the rings spell any six-letter word you please, and snap down the lock upon that, and never a soul can open it—not the maker, even—until somebody comes along that knows the word you snapped it on. Now, Johnny here's goin', and he leaves his drum behind him; for, though he can make pretty music on it, the parchment sags in wet weather, by reason of the sea-water getting at it; an' if he carries it to Plymouth, they'll only condemn it and give him another. And, as for me, I shan't have the heart to put lip to the trumpet any more when Johnny's gone. So we've chosen a word together, and locked 'em together upon that; and, by your leave, I'll hang 'em here together on the hook over your fireplace. Maybe Johnny'll come back; maybe not. Maybe, if he comes, I'll be dead an' gone, an' he'll take 'em apart an' try their music for old sake's sake. But if he never comes, nobody can separate 'em; for nobody beside knows the word. And if you marry and have sons, you can tell 'em that here are tied together the souls of Johnny Christian, drummer of the Marines, and William George Tallifer, once trumpeter of the Queen's Own Hussars. Amen."

‘With that he hung the two instruments 'pon the hook there; and the boy stood up and thanked my father and shook hands; and the pair went forth of the door, towards Helston.

‘Somewhere on the road they took leave of one another; but nobody saw the parting, nor heard what was said between them. About three in the afternoon the trumpeter came walking back over the hill; and by the time my father came home from the fishing, the cottage was tidied up and the tea ready, and the whole place shining like a new pin. From that time for five years he lodged here with my father, looking after the house and tilling the garden; and all the while he was steadily failing, the hurt in his head spreading, in a manner, to his limbs. My father watched the feebleness growing on him, but said nothing. And from first to last neither spake a word about the drummer, John Christian; nor did any letter reach them, nor word of his doings.

'The rest of the tale you'm free to believe, sir, or not, as you please. It stands upon my father's words, and he always declared he was ready to kiss the Book upon it before judge and jury. He said, too, that he never had the wit to make up such a yarn; and he defied anyone to explain about the lock, in particular, by any other tale. But you shall judge for yourself.

'My father said that about three o'clock in the morning, April fourteenth of the year 'fourteen, he and William Tallifer were sitting here, just as you and I, sir, are sitting now. My father had put on his clothes a few minutes before, and was mending his spiller by the light of the horn lantern, meaning to set off before daylight to haul the trammel. The trumpeter hadn't been to bed at all. Towards the last he mostly spent his nights (and his days, too) dozing in the elbow-chair where you sit at this minute. He was dozing then (my father said), with his chin dropped forward on his chest, when a knock sounded upon the door, and the door opened, and in walked an upright young man in scarlet regimentals.

'He had grown a brave bit, and his face was the colour of wood-ashes; but it was the drummer, John Christian. Only his uniform was different from the one he used to wear, and the figures "38" shone in brass upon his collar.

'The drummer walked past my father as if he never saw him, and stood by the elbow-chair and said:

' "Trumpeter, trumpeter, are you one with me?"

'And the trumpeter just lifted the lids of his eyes, and answered, "How should I not be one with you, drummer Johnny—Johnny boy? The men are patient. 'Till you come, I count; while you march, I mark time; until the discharge comes."

' "The discharge has come tonight," said the drummer, "and the word is Corunna no longer"; and stepping to the chimney-place, he unhooked the drum and trumpet, and began to twist the brass rings of the lock, spelling the word aloud, so— C-O-R-U-N-A. When he had fixed the last letter, the padlock opened in his hand.

' "Did you know, trumpeter, that when I came to Plymouth they put me into a line regiment?"

' "The 38th is a good regiment," answered the old Hussar, still in his dull voice. "I went back with them from Sahagun to Corunna. At Corunna they stood in General Fraser's division, on the right. They behaved well."

' "But I'd fain see the Marines again," says the drummer, handing him the trumpet; "and you—you shall call once more for the Queen's Own. Matthew," he says, suddenly, turning on my father—and when he turned, my father saw for the first time that his scarlet jacket had a round hole by the breast-bone, and that the blood was welling there—"Matthew, we shall want your boat."

'Then my father rose on his legs like a man in a dream, while they two slung on, the one his drum, and t'other his trumpet. He took the lantern, and went quaking before them down to the shore, and they breathed heavily behind him; and they stepped into his boat, and my father pushed off.

' "Row you first for Dolor Point," says the drummer. So my father rowed them out past the white houses of Coverack to Dolor Point, and there, at a word, lay on his oars. And the trumpeter, William Tallifer, put his trumpet to his mouth and sounded the *Revelly*. The music of it was like rivers running.

' "They will follow," said the drummer. "Matthew, pull you now for the Manacles."

'So my father pulled for the Manacles, and came to an easy close outside Carn dû. And the drummer took his sticks and beat a tattoo, there by the edge of the reef; and the music of it was like a rolling chariot.

' "That will do," says he, breaking off; "they will follow. Pull now for the shore under Gunner's Meadow."

'Then my father pulled for the shore, and ran his boat in under Gunner's Meadow. And they stepped out, all three, and walked up to the meadow. By the gate the drummer halted and began his tattoo again, looking out towards the darkness over the sea.

'And while the drum beat, and my father held his breath, there came up out of the sea and the darkness a troop of many men, horse and foot, and formed up among the graves; and others rose out of the graves and formed up—drowned Marines with bleached

faces, and pale Hussars riding their horses, all lean and shadowy.
There was no clatter of hoofs or accoutrements, my father said,
but a soft sound all the while, like the beating of a bird's wing,
and a black shadow lying like a pool about the feet of all. The
drummer stood upon a little knoll just inside the gate, and beside
him the tall trumpeter, with hand on hip, watching them gather;
and behind them both my father, clinging to the gate. When no
more came, the drummer stopped playing, and said, "Call the
roll."

Then the trumpeter stepped towards the end man of the rank
and called, "Troop-Sergeant-Major Thomas Irons!" and the man
in a thin voice answered "Here!"

' "Troop-Sergeant-Major Thomas Irons, how is it with you?"

'The man answered, "How should it be with me? When I was
young, I betrayed a girl; and when I was grown, I betrayed a
friend; and for these things I must pay. But I died as a man ought.
God save the King!"

'The trumpeter called to the next man, "Trooper Henry
Buckingham!" and the next man answered, "Here!"

' "Trooper Henry Buckingham, how is it with you?"

' "How should it be with me? I was a drunkard, and I stole,
and in Lugo, in a wine-shop, I knifed a man. But I died as a man
should. God save the King!"

'So the trumpeter went down the line; and when he had finished,
the drummer took it up, hailing the dead Marines in their order.
Each man answered to his name, and each man ended with
"God save the King!" When all were hailed, the drummer
stepped back to his mound, and called:

' "It is well. You are content, and we are content to join you.
Wait yet a little while."

'With this he turned and ordered my father to pick up the
lantern, and lead the way back. As my father picked it up, he
heard the ranks of dead men cheer and call, "God save the King!"
all together, and saw them waver and fade back into the dark,
like a breath fading off a pane.

'But when they came back here to the kitchen, and my father
set the lantern down, it seemed they'd both forgot about him.
For the drummer turned in the lantern-light—and my father
could see the blood still welling out of the hole in his breast—

and took the trumpet-sling from around the other's neck, and locked drum and trumpet together again, choosing the letters on the lock very carefully. While he did this he said:

' "The word is no more Corunna, but Bayonne. As you left out an 'n' in Corunna, so must I leave out an 'n' in Bayonne." And before snapping the padlock, he spelt out the word slowly— "B-A-Y-O-N-E". After that, he used no more speech; but turned and hung the two instruments back on the hook; and then took the trumpeter by the arm; and the pair walked out into the darkness, glancing neither to right nor left.

'My father was on the point of following, when he heard a sort of sigh behind him; and there, sitting in the elbow-chair, was the very trumpeter he had just seen walk out by the door! If my father's heart jumped before, you may believe it jumped quicker now. But after a bit, he went up to the man asleep in the chair, and put a hand upon him. It was the trumpeter in flesh and blood that he touched; but though the flesh was warm, the trumpeter was dead.

'Well, sir, they buried him three days after; and at first my father was minded to say nothing about his dream (as he thought it). But the day after the funeral, he met Parson Kendall coming from Helston market: and the parson called out: "Have 'ee heard the news the coach brought down this mornin'?" "What news?" says my father. "Why, that peace is agreed upon." "None too soon," says my father. "Not soon enough for our poor lads at Bayonne," the parson answered. "Bayonne!" cries my father, with a jump. "Why, yes"; and the parson told him all about a great sally the French had made on the night of April 13th. "Do you happen to know if the 38th Regiment was engaged?" my father asked. "Come, now," said Parson Kendall, "I didn't know you was so well up in the campaign. But, as it happens, I *do* know that the 38th was engaged, for 'twas they that held a cottage and stopped the French advance."

'Still my father held his tongue; and when, a week later, he walked into Helston and bought a *Mercury* off the Sherborne rider, and got the landlord of the "Angel" to spell out the list of killed and wounded, sure enough, there among the killed was Drummer John Christian, of the 38th Foot.

'After this, there was nothing for a religious man but to make a clean breast. So my father went up to Parson Kendall and told the whole story. The parson listened, and put a question or two, and then asked:

' "Have you tried to open the lock since that night?"

' "I han't dared to touch it," says my father.

' "Then come along and try." When the parson came to the cottage here, he took the things off the hook and tried the lock. "Did he say '*Bayonne*'? The word has seven letters."

' "Not if you spell it with one 'n' as *he* did," says my father.

'The parson spelt it out—B-A-Y-O-N-E. "Whew!" says he, for the lock had fallen open in his hand.

'He stood considering it a moment, and then he says, "I tell you what. I shouldn't blab this all round the parish, if I was you. You won't get no credit for truth-telling, and a miracle's wasted on a set of fools. But if you like, I'll shut down the lock again upon a holy word that no one but me shall know, and neither drummer nor trumpeter, dead nor alive, shall frighten the secret out of me."

' "I wish to gracious you would, parson," said my father.

'The parson chose the holy word there and then, and shut the lock back upon it, and hung the drum and trumpet back in their place. He is gone long since, taking the word with him. And till the lock is broken by force, nobody will ever separate those twain.'

SEAN O'CASEY

Deep in Devon

Sean O'Casey (1880–1964), the Irish dramatist, lived from September 1938 to June 1954 at Totnes in Devon. He spent his last ten years at St Marychurch, Torquay. *Sunset and Evening Star* (1954), from which this extract is taken, was the sixth and final volume of his autobiography, begun in 1939 with *I Knock at the Door*.

Devon is almost all a Keltic County, founded by a Keltic tribe which gave its name to the county, a tribe that came over long before the gallant Gaels came sailing over the sea to Eirinn. Another branch of this tribe gave its name to Cornwall. In other ways, Devon tells us the story of her Keltic origin. It is still tinted with the tantalising thoughts of fairy lore. The pishgies or pixies of Devon are brothers to the Gaelic shidhe. They do the same curious things—stealing babies from cradles and leaving change-lings in their place; misleading travellers in the dark; galloping wildly about on the moorland ponies, a minor manner of the Irish pooka. At times they do good things, threshing a farmer's corn for him; but they must be watched, and food, fresh and tasty, must be left for them on the farmhouse floor. A Devon dairy-farmer, well-known to Sean, told him how he had been spellbound one night to the floor of his cattle-shed; how he was surrounded by the pressure of influences hateful and mischievous. He couldn't see but he saw them; couldn't feel, but he felt them; couldn't hear, but he heard them. The flame of his lantern had flickered, gone out, and he stood, stiff and motionless, mid the hot smell from his cattle, his body shivering in the steady trickle of a chilling sweat, his mind trying to move him to the door, his body refusing to stir, so powerless that he couldn't even stretch forth a hand to touch the homely, reassuring body of a cow for comfort, the spiteful influence of some evil thing passing and repassing through him as he stood terrified, body and spirit shaken by the evil influence befouling the byre.

Another farmer told Sean that he had been beset in a contrary way. He had worked in a field all day, and was leaving it in the darkening dusk, but couldn't find the gate that led from the field to the road. He searched where he knew it to be, but it wasn't there; he searched where it might be, but it wasn't there either; he quickened his steps to the quicker beat of his heart, and trotted round the wide field, but saw no sign of a gate, anywhere; anywhere; and the darkness deepened so that he ran round and round the field, probing the hedge here, probing the hedge there; but his fingers touched thorns, the needle-like points of holly leaves, and there was silence everywhere so that the panting of his breast was loud in his ears, coming slower and slower as his legs grew weary, sagging down towards the earth, till he fell down and lay there, fell down flat and lay there still; lay there till the morning came, and they found him senseless, lying stretched out beside the very gate he had sought for throughout the night, in the darkness, under the stars.

As Ireland isn't anything as Irish as some Gaels make her out to be, so England isn't as English as many Irish think her to be. Half of England, and maybe more, is as Keltic as Ireland herself. Listen to the pipe-playing and folk-singing of Northumberland, or to the Cumberland farmers still counting their sheep close to the way the people of Ballyvourney number their scanty flocks. Listen any night to 'Dance Them Around' . . . their band is as Irish as any Ceilidh band in any country town of Ireland. The old songs are neglected and half-forgotten today, and are no longer commonly sung in cottage or farmhouse, just as they are neglected and half-forgotten by Cahersiveen in Kerry and Cushendall in Antrim; though now there is a sleepy interest taken in holding fast to a folk-lore that has almost bidden a picturesque goodbye for ever to the common song a people loves to sing. In listening

one night to a gathering in a village hall, near Leamington, in
Warwickshire, Sean heard an old woman of seventy-four, the
traditional singer of the locality, giving the audience 'Johnny,
My Own True Love', just as he had heard his own mother sing
it in the days of long ago. It was H. G. Wells who, through
Mr Britling Sees It Through voiced delight in the fact that the
bigger part of England's place-names had a Keltic origin; so, what
with all this, with Wales by her side and Scotland over her head,
adding the Irish and their descendants, England is really more
Keltic than the kilt. The old name of London was Caer-Lud, city
of Lugh of the Long Hand, and the city's name today is said to
mean Fort of the Ships, as she, indeed, is to this day; Lydd in
Kent reflects the name of the Irish Lugh, though the English of
today regard the myth with indifference, as do the spiritual and
imaginative Irish. Bud is the name now. Keltic echoes in myth and
story linger on in the countryside throughout Wiltshire,
Somersetshire, Dorsetshire, Devon, and Gloucestershire, up as far
as, and beyond, Northamptonshire, for

> If ever you at Bosworth would be found,
> Then turn your cloaks, for this is fairy ground.

Over the border, a few short miles away, is Cornwall, packed
with the Keltic daylight, with its Derrydown, its Kelly's Round,
its Doloe, meaning two lakes. Here are the Hurlers, remains of
stone circles, called this name because certain Cornishmen persisted
in hurling on Sunday; here are beehive huts, holy wells, and all
the glamorous clutter left by a receding past. It is recorded that a
hundred years ago, West Ireland (Ireland herself) used to play
hurley yearly against East Ireland, comprising the counties of
Devon and Cornwall. Even the story in T. C. Murray's play,
The Wolf, had its origin in a Cornish town. Yet another link was
that of wrestling, or wrastling, as it was called in Dublin; left
hand gripping the shoulder of an opponent, right one gripping
his hip. Cornishmen wrestled in their socks, as did the Irish;
the Devon men in their boots, made as hard as craft could make
them. The reward for an Irish wrestling champion was a coloured
garter worn round the right leg below the knee. Each Sunday, a

champion stood out on a green sward in the Phoenix Park, his trouser leg tucked up to show his gaudy garter, and challenged any among those who crowded round him. Sean's own brother, Michael, wore a garter for a year. The Cornish and Devonian prize was either a silver-plated belt or a gold-laced hat, either of which, earlier on, exempted a wearer from being forced into the Navy.

There is nothing sham about Totnes. Next to London, it is the oldest borough in England. All its 'shoppes' are genuine examples of Tudor or Jacobean housing; not in any way so splendid as those found in Conway or Shrewsbury, but as genuine all the same. Neither is there anything 'arty-crafty' about from the bottom to the top of its hill . . . There are many Irish incidentals about Totnes; the caretaker of the Drill Hall was a Tipperary woman; the owner of a café was another, but now has one in Stoke Gabriel a few short miles away; the plasterer who pasted up new ceilings in the O'Casey house, brought down by bomb concussion, came from Roscommon; the parish priest and the O'Casey family doctor are Dublin men. The one post-woman Totnes had, during the war, came from Tipperary, too. A few miles away, in Brixham, a statue of King Billy stands on the quay, and, like Dublin's old figure, has twice been given a contemptuous coat of football-coloured paint. O'Casey is as relevant in Totnes as he would be in Navan or Kells, and more so than in Dublin now . . .

Totnes is about the size of Mullingar, but busier, wealthier, and much more lively. Apart from the quiet hurry of market day, gentleness is the first quality to give it; gentleness in its buildings, and in the coming and going of its people; and in the slow, winding, winding of the River Dart from the moor to the sea. Oh, lord, the natural lie of it is lovely. Except when visitors pour in during the brief summer, the town is so quiet that it looks like a grey-haired lady, with a young face, sitting calm, hands in lap, unmindful of time, in an orchard of ageing trees, drowsy with the scent of ripened apples about to fall, but which never do; hearing echoes of her own voice in the laughing play of children; or in the whispers of that lover and his lass seeking out some corner of the drowsing orchard that is free from any entanglement of time, care, thought, or casual interference.

Though getting some ready money from summer visitors, the town, like so many Irish ones, depends mainly on the farming communities surrounding it. So the eyes of all often scan the sky—not to see the reality of the sensuous enjoyment of its beauty shown by a Constable, a Ruisdael, or a Turner, but to judge the coming weather, for their livelihood depends on it. In a rainy season, they look for a sign of the sun; in times of undue heat, to catch sight of a hidden cloud. Cattle, sheep, poultry, and crops depend largely on what the sky gives; so, when the sun wears his welcome out, or the rain falls too fulsomely on the land, all eyes search the sky for the chance of a coming change.

An old town, stretching out from Lugh of the Long Hand to Winston Churchill and Clement Attlee, a coming together of a strange god and odd men. Years later, it is said, the Romans came clanking along with spear, short sword, and pilum, the time Julius Caesar was mapping out the way the world should go; but it is doubtful if the Romans pierced farther than Exeter, and, held back by the fighting Kelts, ever had a chance to cool their tired and sweating bodies in the waters of the Dart. Fact or fancy, Totnes is a very ancient borough, stuffed with potent parchments signed by kings and princes, giving it a gorgeous right to live.

Caroline and the Begum

Caroline Fox of Falmouth (1819–71), of the famous Cornish Quaker family, kept a valuable set of journals. They were selectively edited by Wendy Monk in 1972.

Falmouth, December 2, 1836—We called at Pearce's Hotel on the Begum of Oude who is leaving England (where her husband is ambassador) on a pilgrimage to Mecca. Her bright little Hindustani maid told us she was 'gone down cappin's'; so to Captain Clavel's we followed her and spent a most amusing half-hour in her society. She was seated in great state in the midst of the family circle, talking English with great self-possession in spite of her charming blunders. Her dress was an immense pair of trousers of striped Indian silk, a Cashmere shawl laid over her head, over a close covering of blue and yellow silk, two pairs of remarkable slippers, numbers of anklets and leglets, a great deal of jewellery, and a large blue cloak over all. She was very conversable, showed us her ornaments, wrote her name and title in English and Arabic in my book, and offered to make an egg curry. At the top of the page where she wrote her name she inscribed in Arabic sign 'Allah', saying, 'That name God you take great care of.' She sat by Mrs Clavel, and after petting and stroking her for a while, declared, 'Love I you.' She promised her and Leonora a Cashmere shawl apiece, adding, 'I get them very cheap, five shillings, seven shillings, ten shillings, very good, for I daughter king, duty take I, tell merchants my, make shawls, and I send you and miss.' She has spent a year in London, her name is Miriam and her husband's Molvè Mohammed Ishmael. Her face is one of quick sagacity but extreme ugliness.

December 3—The next day we found her squatting on her bed on the floor, an idiot servant of the Prophet in a little heap in one corner, her black-eyed handmaiden grinning us a welcome, and a sacred kitten frolicking over the trappings of Eastern state. We were most graciously received with a shriek of pleasure. Her observations on English life were very entertaining. She told us of going to 'the Court of the King of London.—He very good man, but he no power.—Parliament all power.—King no give half-penny but call Parliament, make council, council give leave, King give half-penny.—For public charity King give one sovereign, poor little shopman, baker-man, fish-man, barter-man also give one sovereign. Poor King!—King Oude he give one thousand rupees, palanquin mans with gold stick, elephants, camels: no ask Parliament.' She and Papa [Robert Were Fox] talked a little theology, she of course began it. 'I believe but one God, very bad not to think so; you believe Jesus Christ was prophet?' Papa said, 'Not a prophet, but the Son of God.' 'How you think so, God Almighty never marry! In London every one go to ball, theatre, dance, sing, walk, read; no go Mecca. I mind not that, I go Mecca, I very good woman.' She took a great fancy to Barclay [Caroline's brother], declaring him very like her son. She offered him a commission in the King of Oude's army and £1,200 a year if he would come over and be her son; she gave him a rupee, probably as bounty money. There are 200 English in her King's service, two doctors, and three aides-de-camp. She showed us some magnificent jewellery, immense pearls, diamonds, and emeralds, tied up so carelessly in a dirty handker-chief. Her armlets were very curious, and she had a silver ring on her great toe which lay in no obscurity before her. Then a number of her superb dresses were displayed, gold and silver tissues, satins, cashmeres, muslins of an almost impossible thinness, which she is going to give away at Mecca. She is aunt to the present, sister of the late, and daughter of the former, King of Oude. She has a stone house in which she keeps fifteen Persian cats. It is a great virtue to keep cats, and a virtue with infinite reward attached, to keep an idiot: the one with her here she discovered in London, and was very glad to appropriate the little Eastern mystery. Aunt Charles's bonnet amused her, she wanted to know if it was a new fashion; she talked of the Quakers, and said they were honest and never told lies.

December 5—Today the Begum began almost at once on theology, asking mamma if 'she were a *religieuse*', and then began to expound her own creed. She took the Koran and read some passages, then an English psalm containing similar sentiments, then she chanted a Mahometan collect beautifully in Arabic and Hindustani. She made mamma write all our names that she might send us a letter, and then desired Aunt Lucy to write something, the purport of which it was not easy to divine. At last she explained herself, 'Say what you think of Marriam Begum, say she religious, or she bad woman, or whatever you think.' Poor Aunt Lucy could not refuse, and accordingly looked sapient, bit her pen-stump, and behold the precipitate from this strong acid, 'We have been much interested in seeing Marriam Begum, and think her a religious lady.' I think a moral chemist would pronounce this to be the result of more alkali than acid, but it was an awkward corner to be driven into. She was coming to visit us today, but had to embark instead, after expressing her hopes that we should meet again in Oude!

December 28—On coming home this morning, found Molvè Mohammed, the Begum's husband, and his secretary, in the drawing-room. He has a sensible face, not totally unlike his wife's and was dressed in the English costume. On showing him the Begum's writing in my book, he was much pleased at her having inserted his name as an introduction to her own. 'Ha! she no forget, I very glad see that.' He added some writing of his own in Persian, the sense of which was, 'When I was young I used to

hunt tigers and lions, but my intercourse with the ladies of England
has driven all that out of my head.' He is said to be by no means
satisfied with bigamy, and it is added that one of the motives of
the Begum's English visit was to collect wives for the King of
Oude . . .

THOMAS HARDY

Rumour in Wessex

Thomas Hardy, in his sixties, between 1903 and 1908, wrote *The Dynasts*, a vast 'epic-drama of the war with Napoleon, in three Parts, nineteen Acts, and one hundred and thirty Scenes'. He said in his preface: 'The Spectacle here presented in the likeness of a Drama is concerned with the Great Historical Calamity, or Clash of Peoples, artificially brought about some hundred years ago.'

Though he did not intend it for the theatre (about which he was always engagingly innocent), portions of it have been acted. Harley Granville Barker staged certain scenes at the Kingsway, London, in the autumn of 1914, and the Oxford University Dramatic Society presented it in Oxford during February 1920, with Hardy himself present. Some years after his death the play found on radio a fitting stage of the imagination, especially in the adaptation (1944) by Dallas Bower, produced by Val Gielgud. In September 1980 Crispin Thomas directed scenes in Exeter Cathedral.

The Dynasts offers an astonishing assemblage of styles: blank verse, prose, and rhyme in various metrical patterns. Behind the Napoleonic narrative is a complicated philosophical framework of creation and fate, with its 'phantasmal Intelligences'. Stage directions throughout are splendidly expressive.

The scene below, fifth in the second act of the first Part, is from Hardy's Wessex in the summer of 1805 at an hour when invasion was expected daily and rumour swept the land. Hardy had a note: 'The remains of the lonely hut occupied by the beacon-keepers, consisting of some half-buried brickbats, and a little mound of peat, over-grown with moss, are still visible on the elevated spot referred to. The two keepers themselves, and their eccentricities and sayings, are traditionary, with a slight disguise of names.'

ACT II SCENE V

RAINBARROW'S BEACON, EGDON HEATH

Night in mid-August, 1805. A lofty ridge of heathland reveals itself dimly, terminating in an abrupt slope, at the summit of which are three tumuli. On the sheltered side of the most prominent of them stands a hut of turves with a brick chimney. In front are two ricks of fuel, one of heather and furze for quick ignition, the other of wood, for slow burning. Something in the feel of the darkness and in the personality of the spot imparts a sense of uninterrupted space around, the view by day extending from the cliffs of the Isle of Wight eastward to Blackdon Hill by Dead-man's Bay westward, and south across the Valley of the Froom to the ridge that screens the Channel.

Two men with pikes loom up, on duty as beacon-keepers beside the ricks.

OLD MAN

Now, Jems Purchess, once more mark my words. Black'on is the point we've to watch, and not Kingsbere; and I'll tell'ee for why. If he do land anywhere hereabout 'twill be inside Deadman's Bay, and the signal will straightway come from Black'on. But there thou'st stand, glowering and staring with all thy eyes at Kingsbere! I tell 'ee what 'tis, Jem Purchess, your brain is softening; and you be getting too old for business of state like ours!

YOUNG MAN

You've let your tongue wrack your few rames of good breeding, John.

OLD MAN

The words of my Lord-Lieutenant was, whenever you see Kingsbere-Hill Beacon fired to the eastward, or Black'on to the westward, light up; and keep your second fire burning for two hours. Was that our documents or was it not?

YOUNG MAN

I don't gainsay it. And so I keep my eye on Kingsbere, because that's most likely o' the two, says I.

OLD MAN

That shows the curious depths of your ignorance. However, I'll have patience, and say on. Didst ever larn geography?

YOUNG MAN

No. Nor no other corrupt practices.

OLD MAN

Tcht-tcht!—Well, I'll have patience, and put it to him in another form. Dost know the world is round—eh? I warrant dostn't!

YOUNG MAN

I warrant I do!

OLD MAN

How d'ye make that out, when th'st never been to school?

YOUNG MAN

I larned it at church, thank God.

OLD MAN

Church? What have God A'mighty got to do with profane knowledge? Beware that you baint blaspheming, Jems Purchess!

YOUNG MAN

I say I did, whether or no! 'Twas the zingers up in gallery that I had it from. They busted out that strong with 'the round world and they that dwell therein', that we common fokes down under could do no less than believe 'em.

OLD MAN

Canst be sharp enough in the wrong place as usual—I warrant canst! However, I'll have patience with 'en, and say on!—Suppose, now, my hat is the world; and there, as might be, stands the Camp of Belong, where Boney is. The world goes round, so, and Belong goes round too. Twelve hours pass; round goes the world still—so. Where's Belong now?

A pause. Two other figures, a man's and a woman's, rise against the sky out of the gloom.

OLD MAN (*shouldering his pike*)
Who goes there? Friend or foe, in the King's name!

WOMAN
Piece o' trumpery! 'Who goes' yourself! What d'ye talk o', John Whiting! Can't your eyes earn their living any longer, then, that you don't know your own neighbours? 'Tis Private Cantle of the Locals and his wife Keziar, down at Bloom's-End—who else should it be!

OLD MAN (*lowering his pike*)
A form o' words, Mis'ess Cantle, no more; ordained by his Majesty's Gover'ment to be spoke by all we on sworn duty for the defence o' the country. Strict rank-and-file rules is our only horn of salvation in these times.—But, my dear woman, why ever have ye come lumpering up to Rainbarrows at this time o' night?

WOMAN
We've been troubled with bad dreams, owing to the firing out at sea yesterday; and at last I could sleep no more, feeling sure that sommat boded of His coming. And I said to Cantle, I'll ray myself, and go up to Beacon, and ask if anything have been heard or seen tonight. And here we be.

OLD MAN
Not a sign or sound—all's as still as a churchyard. And how is your good man?

PRIVATE (*advancing*)
Clk! I be all right! I was in the ranks, helping to keep the ground at the review by the King this week. We was a wonderful sight—wonderful! The King said so again and again.—Yes, there was he,

and there was I, though not daring to move a' eyebrow in the presence of Majesty. I have come home on a night's leave—off there again tomorrow. Boney's expected every day, the Lord be praised! Yes, our hopes are to be fulfilled soon, as we say in the army.

OLD MAN

There, there, Cantle; don't ye speak quite so large, and stand so over-upright. Your back is as holler as a fire-dog's. Do ye suppose that we on active service here don't know war news? Mind you don't go taking to your heels when the next alarm comes, as you did at last year's.

PRIVATE

That had nothing to do with fighting, for I'm as bold as a lion when I'm up, and 'Shoulder Fawlocks!' sounds as common as my own name to me. 'Twas— (*Lowering his voice.*) Have ye heard?

OLD MAN

To be sure we have.

PRIVATE

Ghastly, isn't it!

OLD MAN

Ghastly! Frightful!

YOUNG MAN (*to Private*)

He don't know what it is! That's his pride and puffery. What is it that's so ghastly—hey?

PRIVATE

Well, there, I can't tell it. 'Twas that that made the whole eighty of our company run away—though we be the bravest of the brave in natural jeopardies, or the little boys wouldn't run after us and call us the 'Bang-up-Locals'.

WOMAN (*in undertones*)

I can tell you a word or two on't. It is about His victuals. They say that He lives upon human flesh, and has rashers o' baby every morning for breakfast—for all the world like the Cernel Giant in old ancient times!

YOUNG MAN

Ye can't believe all ye hear.

PRIVATE

I only believe half. And I only own—such is my challengeful character—that perhaps He do eat pagan infants when He's in the desert. But not Christian ones at home. Oh no—'tis too much.

WOMAN

Whether or no, I sometimes—God forgie me!—laugh wi' horror at the queerness o't, till I am that weak I can hardly go round house. He should have the washing of 'em a few times; I warrant 'a wouldn't want to eat babies any more!

A silence, during which they gaze around at the dark dome of starless sky.

YOUNG MAN

There'll be a change in the weather soon, by the look o't. I can hear the cows moo in Froom Valley as if I were close to 'em, and the lantern at Max Turnpike is shining quite plain.

OLD MAN

Well, come in and taste a drop o' sommat we've got here, that will warm the cockles of your heart as ye wamble homealong. We housed eighty tubs last night for them that shan't be named —landed at Lullwind Cove the night afore, though they had a narrow shave with the riding-officers this run.

They make towards the hut, when a light on the west horizon becomes visible, and quickly enlarges.

YOUNG MAN

He's come!

OLD MAN

Come he is, though you do say it! This, then, is the beginning of what England's waited for!

They stand and watch the light awhile.

YOUNG MAN

Just what you was praising the Lord for by-now, Private Cantle.

PRIVATE

My meaning was——

WOMAN (*simpering*)

Oh that I hadn't married a fiery sojer, to make me bring fatherless children into the world, all through his dreadful calling! Why didn't a man of no sprawl content me!

OLD MAN (*shouldering his pike*)

We can't heed your innocent pratings any longer, good neighbours, being in the King's service, and a hot invasion on. Fall in, fall in, mate. Straight to the tinder-box. Quick march!

The two men hasten to the hut, and are heard striking a flint and steel. Returning with a lit lantern they ignite a wisp of furze, and with this set the first stack of fuel in a blaze. The private of the Locals and his wife hastily retreat by the light of the flaming beacon, under which the purple rotundities of the heath show like bronze, and the pits like the eye-sockets of a skull.

SPIRIT SINISTER

This is good, and spells blood: (*To the Chorus of the Years.*) I assume that It means to let us carry out this invasion with pleasing slaughter, so as not to disappoint my hope?

SEMI-CHORUS I OF THE YEARS (*aerial music*)
We carry out? Nay, but should we
Ordain what bloodshed is to be!

SEMI–CHORUS II

The Immanent, that urgeth all,
Rules what may or may not befall!

SEMI–CHORUS I

Ere systemed suns were globed and lit
The slaughters of the race were writ,

SEMI–CHORUS II

And wasting wars, by land and sea,
Fixed, like all else, immutably!

SPIRIT SINISTER

Well; be it so. My argument is that War makes rattling good
history; but Peace is poor reading. So I back Bonaparte for the
reason that he will give pleasure to posterity.

SPIRIT OF THE PITIES

Gross hypocrite!

CHORUS OF THE YEARS

We comprehend him not.

*The day breaks over the heathery upland, on which the beacon is still
burning. The morning reveals the white surface of a highway which,
coming from the royal watering-place beyond the hills, stretches towards
the outskirts of the heath and passes away eastward.*

DUMB SHOW

*Moving figures and vehicles dot the surface of the road, all progressing
in one direction, away from the coast. In the foreground the shapes
appear as those of civilians, mostly on foot, but many in gigs and trades-
men's carts and on horseback. When they reach an intermediate hill
some pause and look back; others enter on the next decline landwards
without turning their heads.*

From the opposite horizon numerous companies of volunteers, in the *local uniform of red with green facings,* are moving coastwards in companies; as are also irregular bodies of pikemen without uniform; while on the upper slopes of the downs towards the shore regiments of the line are visible, with cavalry and artillery; all passing over to the coast.*

At a signal from the Chief Intelligences two Phantoms of Rumour enter on the highway in the garb of country-men.

FIRST PHANTOM (*to Pedestrians*)
Whither so fast, good neighbours, and before breakfast, too?
Empty bellies be bad to vamp on.

FIRST PEDESTRIAN (*laden with a pack, and speaking breathlessly*)
He's landed west'ard, out by Abbot's Beach. And if you have property you'll save it and yourselves, as we are doing!

SECOND PEDESTRIAN
All yesterday the firing at Boulogne
Was like the seven thunders heard in Heaven
When the fierce angel spoke. So did he draw
Men's eyes that way, the while his thousand boats
Full-manned, flat-bottomed for the shallowest shore,
Dropped down to west, and crossed our frontage here.
Seen from above they specked the water-shine
As will a flight of swallows towards dim eve,
Descending on a smooth and loitering stream
To seek some eyot's sedge.

SECOND PHANTOM
We are sent to enlighten you and ease your souls.
Even now a courier canters to the port
To check the baseless scare.

FIRST PEDESTRIAN (*to Second Pedestrian*)
These be inland men who, I warrant 'ee, don't know a lerret

---

*These historic facings, which, I believe, won for the local (old 39th) regiment the nickname of 'Green Linnets', have been changed for no apparent reason. (They are now restored.—1909.)

from a lighter! Let's take no heed of such, comrade; and hurry on!

FIRST PHANTOM
                    Will you not hear
That what was seen behind the midnight mist,
Their oar-blades tossing twinkles to the moon,
Was but a fleet of fishing-craft belated
By reason of the vastness of their haul?

FIRST PEDESTRIAN

Hey? And d'ye know it?—Now I look back to the top o'
Rudgeway the folk do seem as come to a pause there.—Be this
true, never again do I stir my stumps for any alarm short of the
Day of Judgment! Nine times has my rheumatical rest been
broke in these last three years by hues and cries of Boney upon us.
'Od rot the feller; now he's made a fool of me once more, till
my inside is like a wash-tub, what wi' being so gallied, and
running so leery!—But how if you be one of the enemy, sent to
sow these tares, so to speak it, these false tidings, and coax us into
a fancied safety? Hey, neighbours? I don't, after all, care for this
story!

SECOND PEDESTRIAN
              Onwards again!
If Boney's come, 'tis best to be away;
And if he's not, why, we've a holiday!

Exeunt Pedestrians.

*The Spirits of Rumour vanish, while the scene seems to become
involved in the smoke from the beacon, and slowly disappears.*

W. M. THACKERAY

Theatre Royal, Chatteris

Chatteris, in William Makepeace Thackeray's novel, *Pendennis* (1849), is Exeter in the 1830s. *The Stranger*, in which Miss Fotheringay appears, is Benjamin Thompson's version of a German play by Kotzebue. Dolphin, the London impresario, can be identified with Alfred Bunn, the brisk vulgarian who in his day was manager of both Covent Garden and Drury Lane. He was the librettist of *The Bohemian Girl*. Foker is a friend of Arthur Pendennis.

They moved off to the theatre, where they paid their money to the wheezy old lady slumbering in the money-taker's box. 'Mrs Dropsicum, Bingley's mother-in-law, great in Lady Macbeth,' Foker said to his companion.

They had almost their choice of places in the boxes of the theatre, which was no better filled than country theatres usually are in spite of the 'universal burst of attraction and galvanic thrills of delight' advertised by Bingley in the playbills. A score or so of people dotted the pit-benches, a few more kept a kicking and whistling in the galleries, and a dozen others, who came in with free admissions, were in the boxes where our young gentlemen sate. Lieutenants Rodgers and Podgers, and young Cornet Tidmus, of the Dragoons, occupied a private box. The performers acted to them, and these gentlemen seemed to hold conversation with the players when not engaged in the dialogue, and applauded them by name loudly.

Bingley, the manager, who assumed all the chief comic and tragic parts except when he modestly retreated to make way for the London stars who came down occasionally to Chatteris, was great in the character of the 'Stranger'. He was attired in the tight pantaloons and Hessian boots which the stage legion has given to that injured man, with a large cloak and beaver and a hearse-feather in it drooping over his raddled old face, and only partially concealing his great buckled brown wig. He had the stage-jewellery on too, of which he selected the largest and most shiny rings for himself, and allowed his little finger to quiver out of his cloak with a sham diamond ring covering the first joint of the finger, and twiddling in the faces of the pit. Bingley made it a favour to the young men of his company to go on in light comedy parts with that ring. They flattered him by asking its history. The stage has its traditional jewels, as the Crown and all great families have. This had belonged to George Frederick Cooke, who had had it from Mr Quin, who may have bought it for a shilling. Bingley fancied the world was fascinated with its glitter.

He was reading out of the stage-book—that wonderful stage-book—which is not bound like any other book in the world, but is rouged and tawdry like the hero or heroine who holds it, as people never do hold books; and points with his finger to a passage, and wags his head ominously at the audience, and then lifts up eyes and finger to the ceiling, professing to derive some intense consolation from the work between which and heaven there is a strong affinity.

As soon as the Stranger saw the young men he acted at them; eyeing them solemnly over his gilt volume as he lay on the stage-bank showing his hand, his ring and his Hessians. He calculated the effect that every one of these ornaments would produce upon his victims; he was determined to fascinate them, for he knew they had paid their money; and he saw their families coming in from the country and filling the cane chairs in his boxes.

As he lay on the bank reading, his servant, Francis, made remarks upon (and to) his master . . .

Francis: Hope is the nurse of life.
Bingley: And her cradle—is the grave.

The Stranger uttered this with the moan of a bassoon in agony, and fixed his glance on Pendennis so steadily that the poor lad was quite put out of countenance. He thought the whole house must be looking at him; and cast his eyes down. As soon as ever he raised them Bingley's were at him again. All through the scene the manager played at him. How relieved the lad was when the scene ended, and Foker, tapping with his cane, cried out 'Bravo, Bingley!'

'Give him a hand, Pendennis; you know every chap likes a hand,' Mr Foker said; and the good-natured young gentleman, and Pendennis laughing, and the Dragoons in the opposite box, began clapping hands to the best of their power.

A chamber in Wintersen Castle closed over Tobias's hut and the Stranger and his boots; and servants appeared bustling about with chairs and tables—'That's Hicks and Miss Thackthwaite,' whispered Foker, 'Pretty girl, ain't she, Pendennis? But stop—hurray—bravo! here's the Fotheringay.'

The pit thrilled and thumped its umbrellas; a volley of applause was fired from the gallery; the Dragoon officers and Foker clapped their hands furiously; you would have thought the house was full, so loud were their plaudits . . . Pen's eyes opened wide and bright, as Mrs Haller entered with a downcast look, then rallying at the sound of the applause, swept the house with a grateful glance, and, folding her hands across her breast, sank down in a magnificent curtsey. More applause, more umbrellas; Pen this time, flaming with wine and enthusiasm, clapped hands and sang 'Bravo' louder than all. Mrs Haller saw him; and everybody else; and old Mr Bows, the little first fiddler of the orchestra (which was this night increased by a detachment of the band of the Dragoons, by the kind permission of Colonel Swallowtail), looked up from the desk where he was perched, with his crutch beside him, and smiled at the enthusiasm of the lad.

Those who have only seen Miss Fotheringay in later days, since her marriage and introduction into London life, have little idea how beautiful a creature she was at the time when our friend Pen first set eyes on her. She was of the tallest of women, and at her then age of six-and-twenty—for six-and-twenty she was, though she vowed she was only nineteen—in the prime and fullness of her beauty . . . She was dressed in long flowing robes of black, which she managed and swept to and fro with wonderful grace, and out of the folds of which you only saw her sandals occasionally; they were of rather a large size; but Pen thought them as ravishing as the slippers of Cinderella . . .

She stood for a moment—complete and beautiful—as Pen stared at her. 'I say, Pen, isn't she a stunner?' asked Mr Foker.

'Hush!' Pen said, 'She's speaking.'

She began her business in a deep sweet voice. Those who know the play of *The Stranger* are aware that the remarks made by the various characters are not valuable in themselves, either for their sound sense, their novelty of observation, or their poetic fancy.

Nobody ever talked so . . . The Stranger's talk is sham, like the book he reads, and the hair he wears, and the bank he sits on, and the diamond ring he makes play with—but, in the midst of the balderdash, there runs that reality of love, children, and forgiveness of wrong, which will be listened to wherever it is preached, and sets all the world sympathising.

With what smothered sorrow, with what gushing pathos, Mrs Haller delivered her part! At first, when as Count Wintersen's housekeeper and preparing for his Excellency's arrival, she had to give orders about the beds and furniture, and the dinner, etc., to be got ready, she did so with the calm agony of despair. But when she could get rid of the stupid servants, and give vent to her feelings to the pit and the house, she overflowed to each individual as if he were her particular confidant, and she was crying out her grief on his shoulder; the little fiddler in the orchestra (whom she did not seem to watch, though he followed her ceaselessly), twitched, twisted, nodded, pointed about, and when she came to the favourite passage, 'I have a William, too, if he be still alive—Ah, yes, if he be still alive. His little sisters, too. Why, Fancy, dost thou rack me so? Why dost thou image my poor children fainting in sickness, and crying to—to their mum-um-other',—when she came to this passage little Bows buried his face in his blue cotton handkerchief, after crying out 'Bravo!'

All the house was affected. Foker, for his part, taking out a large yellow bandanna, wept piteously. As for Pen, he was gone too far for that. He followed the woman about and about—when she was off the stage, it and the house were blank; the lights and the red officers reeled wildly before his sight. He watched her at the side-scene—where she stood waiting to come on the stage, and where her father took off her shawl: when the reconciliation arrived, and she flung herself down on Mr Bingley's shoulders, whilst the children clung to their knees, and the Countess (Mrs Bingley) and Baron Steinforth (performed with great liveliness and spirit by Garbetts)—while the rest of the characters formed a group round them, Pen's hot eyes saw only Fotheringay, Fotheringay. The curtain fell upon him like a pall. He did not hear a word of what Bingley said, who came forward to announce the play for the next evening, and who took the tumultuous applause, as usual, for himself. Pen was not even distinctly aware that the house was calling for Miss Fotheringay, nor did the manager seem to comprehend that anyone else had caused the success of the play. At last he understood it—stepped back with a grin, and presently appeared with Mrs Haller on his arm. How beautiful she looked! Her hair had fallen down, the officers threw her flowers. She clutched them to her heart. She put back her hair, and smiled all round. Her eyes met Pen's. Down went the curtain again, and she was gone. Not one note could be heard of the overture which the brass band of the Dragoons blew by kind permission of Colonel Swallowtail.

'She *is* a crusher, ain't she now?' Mr Foker asked of his companion.

Pen did not know exactly what Foker said, and answered vaguely. He could not tell the other what he felt; he could not have spoken, just then, to any mortal. Besides, Pendennis did not quite know what he felt yet; it was something overwhelming, maddening, delicious; a fever of wild joy and undefined longing.

And now Rowkins and Miss Thackthwaite came on to dance the favourite double hornpipe, and Foker abandoned himself to the delights of this ballet, just as he had to the tears of the tragedy, a few minutes before. Pen did not care for it, or indeed think about the dance, except to remember that that woman was acting with her in the scene where she first came in. It was a mist before his eyes. At the end of the dance he looked at his watch and said it was time for him to go.

'Hang it, stay to see "The Bravo of the Battle-Axe",' Foker said, 'Bingley's splendid in it; he wears red tights, and has to carry Mrs B. over the Pine-bridge of the Cataract, only she's too heavy. It's great fun, do stop.'

Pen looked at the bill with one lingering fond hope that Miss Fotheringay's name might be hidden, somewhere, in the list of the actors of the after-piece, but there was no such name. Go he must. He had a long ride home. He squeezed Foker's hand. He was choking to speak, but he couldn't. He quitted the theatre and walked frantically about the town, he knew not how long; then he mounted at the George and rode homewards, and Clavering [Ottery St Mary] clock sang out one as he came into the yard at Fairoaks.

[Pendennis is in love. He meets the Fotheringay in her lodgings (her father is a shabby 'Captain') in 'that quiet little street in Chatteris, called Prior's Lane, which lies close by Dean's Green and the canons' houses, and is overlooked by the enormous towers of the cathedral'. Later he sees her as Ophelia]

Mr Hornbull, from London, was the Hamlet of the night, Mr Bingley modestly contenting himself with the part of Horatio, and reserving his chief strength for William in *Black-Eyed Susan*, which was the second piece.

We have nothing to do with the play; except to say that Ophelia looked lovely, and performed with admirable wild pathos: laughing, weeping, gazing wildly, waving her beautiful white arms, and flinging about her snatches of flowers and songs with the most charming madness. What an opportunity her splendid black hair had of tossing over her shoulders! She made the most charming corpse ever seen; and while Hamlet and Laertes were battling in her grave, she was looking out from the back scenes with some curiosity towards Pen's box, and the family party assembled in it . . .

When the curtain fell upon that group of slaughtered personages who are dispatched so suddenly at the end of *Hamlet*, there was an immense shouting and applause from all quarters of the house . . . Pen bellowing with the loudest, 'Fotheringay! Fotheringay!', Messrs Spavin and Foker giving the view halloo from their box.

Hornbull led the *bénéficiare* forward amidst bursts of enthusiasm—
and she looked so handsome and radiant, with her hair still over
her shoulders, that Pen could hardly contain himself for rapture . . .
As for Miss Fotheringay, she surveyed the house all round with
glances of gratitude; and trembled, and almost sank with emotion,
over her favourite trap-door. She seized the flowers and pressed
them to her swelling heart, &c, &c . . .

Black-Eyed Susan followed, at which sweet story our gentle-
hearted friends were exceedingly charmed and affected; and in
which Susan, with a russet gown and a pink ribbon in her cap,
looked to the full as lovely as Ophelia. Bingley was great in
William; Goll, as the Admiral, looked like the figurehead of a
seventy-four; and Garbetts, as Captain Boldweather, a miscreant
who forms a plan for carrying off Black-Eyed Susan, and waving
an immense cocked hat, says, 'Come what may, he *will* be the
ruin of her'—all these performed their parts with their accustomed
talent; and it was with a sincere regret that our friends saw the
curtain drop down and end that pretty and tender story.

[Pendennis becomes deeply involved; but his uncle copes with
the affair; and, in any event, the Fotheringay has a call to
London. An important manager visits the Chatteris theatre.]

Mr Manager Bingley was performing his famous character of
Rolla in *Pizarro* to a house so exceedingly thin that it would
appear as if the part of Rolla was by no means such a favourite
with the people of Chatteris as it was with the accomplished actor
himself. Scarce anybody was in the theatre. Poor Pen had the
boxes almost to himself, and sate there lonely, with bloodshot
eyes, leaning over the ledge and gazing haggardly towards the
scene, when Cora came in. When she was not on the stage, he
saw nothing. Spaniards and Peruvians, processions and battles,
priests and virgins of the sun, went in and out, and had their talk,
but Arthur took no note of any one of them; and only saw Cora
whom his soul longed after . . . There he sate then, miserable, and
gazing at her. And she took no more notice of him than he did
of the rest of the house.

The Fotheringay was uncommonly handsome, in a white
raiment and leopard skin, with a sun upon her breast, and fine

tawdry bracelets on her beautiful glancing arms. She spouted the
few words of her part, and looked it still better. The eyes, which
had overthrown Pen's soul, rolled and gleamed as lustrous as ever;
but it was not to him that they were directed that night. He did
not know to who, or remark a couple of gentlemen, in the box
next to him, upon whom Miss Fotheringay's glances were
perpetually shining.

Nor had Pen noticed the extraordinary change which had
taken place on the stage a short time after the entry of these two
gentlemen into the theatre. There were so few people in the house
that the first act of the play languished entirely, and there had
been some question of returning the money. The actors were
perfectly careless about their parts, and yawned through the
dialogue, and talked loud to each other in the intervals. Even
Bingley was listless, and Mrs B. in Elvira spoke under her breath.

How came it that all of a sudden Mrs Bingley began to raise
her voice and bellow like a bull of Bashan? Whence was it that
Bingley, flinging off his apathy, darted about the stage and yelled
like Kean? Why did Garbetts and Rowkins and Miss Rouncy try,
each of them, the force of their charms or graces, and act and
swagger and scowl and speak their very loudest at the two
gentlemen in box No 3?

One was a quiet little man in black, with a grey head and a
jolly, shrewd face—the other was in all respects a splendid and
remarkable individual. He was a tall and portly gentleman with a
hooked nose and a profusion of curling brown hair and whiskers;
his coat was covered with the richest frogs, braidings, and velvet.
He had under-waistcoats, many splendid rings, jewelled pins, and
neck-chains. When he took out his yellow pocket-handkerchief
with his hand that was cased in white kids, a delightful odour of
musk and bergamot was shaken through the house. He was
evidently a personage of rank, and it was to him that the little
Chatteris company was acting.

He was, in a word, no other than Mr Dolphin, the great manager
from London, accompanied by his faithful friend and secretary Mr
William Minns; without whom he never travelled. He had not
been ten minutes in the theatre before his august presence there
was perceived by Bingley and the rest; and they all began to act
their best and try to engage his attention. Even Miss Fotheringay's

dull heart, which was disturbed at nothing, felt, perhaps, a flutter when she came in the presence of the famous London Impresario. She had not much to do in her part, but to look handsome, and stand in picturesque attitudes encircling her child; and she did this work to admiration. In vain the various actors tried to win the favour of the great stage Sultan. Pizarro bellowed, and the Manager only took snuff out of his great gold box. It was only in the last scene when Rolla comes in staggering with the infant (Bingley is not so strong as he was, and his fourth son Master Talma Bingley is a monstrous large child for his age)—when Rolla comes staggering with the child to Cora, who rushes forward with a shriek and says—'O God, there's blood upon him!'—that the London manager clapped his hands, and broke out with an enthusiastic bravo.

Then, having concluded his applause, Mr Dolphin gave his secretary a clap on the shoulder, and said, 'by Jove, Billy, she'll do.'

'Who taught her that dodge?' said old Billy, who was a sardonic old gentleman—'I remember her at the Olympic, and hang me if she could say Bo to a goose.'

It was little Mr Bows in the orchestra who had taught her the 'dodge' in question. All the company heard the applause, and, as the curtain went down, came round her, and congratulated and hated Miss Fotheringay.

[Dolphin was in the audience because of a neat diplomatic exercise by Pendennis's uncle. Clearly, for the boy's sake, the Fotheringay should leave Chatteris; and the wisest way was to interest the great Marquis of Steyne.]

'It is the nephew's affair, depend upon it,' said the Marquis. 'The young man is in a scrape. I was myself—when I was in the fifth form at Eton—a market-gardener's daughter—and swore I'd marry her. I was mad about her—poor Polly!' Here he made a pause, and perhaps the past rose up to Lord Steyne, and George Gaunt was a boy again not altogether lost. 'But I say, she must be a fine woman from Pendennis's account. Have in Dolphin, and let us hear if he knows anything of her.' . . .

The visit to Chatteris was the result of their conversation; and Mr Dolphin wrote to his Lordship from that place, and did himself the honour to inform the Marquis of Steyne that he had seen the lady about whom his Lordship had spoken, that he was as much struck by her talent as he was by her personal appearance, and that he had made an engagement with Miss Fotheringay, who would soon have the honour of appearing before a London audience, and his noble and enlightened patron, the Marquis of Steyne.

Pen read the announcement of Miss Fotheringay's engagement in the Chatteris paper where he had so often praised her charms. The editor made very handsome mention of her talent and beauty, and prophesied her success in the metropolis. Bingley, the manager, began to advertise 'The last night of Miss Fotheringay's engagement.' Poor Pen and Sir Derby Oaks were very constant at the play; Sir Derby in the stage-box, throwing bouquets and getting glances—Pen in the almost deserted boxes, haggard, wretched, and lonely. Nobody cared whether Miss Fotheringay was going or staying except those two—and perhaps one more, which was Mr Bows of the orchestra.

He came out of his place one night, and went into the house to the box where Pen was; and he held out his hand to him, and asked him to come and walk. They walked down the street together; and went and sate upon Chatteris bridge in the moonlight, and talked about Her. 'We may sit on the same bridge,' said he: 'We have been in the same boat for a long time. You are not the only man who has made a fool of himself about that woman. And I have less excuse than you because I'm older and know her better. She has no more heart than the stone you are leaning on; and it is you or I might fall into the water, and never come up again, and she wouldn't care. Yes—she would care for me, and will be forced to send to me from London. But she wouldn't if she didn't want me. She has no heart and no head, and no sense, and no feelings, and no griefs or cares, whatever. I was going to say no pleasures—but the fact is she does like her dinner, and she is pleased when people admire her.'

'And you do?' said Pen, interested out of himself, and wondering at the crabbed homely little old man.

'It's a habit, like taking snuff, or drinking drams,' said the other. 'It was I made her. If she doesn't send for me, I shall follow her; but I know she'll send for me. She wants me. Some day she'll marry, and fling me over, as I do the end of this cigar.'

The little flaming spark dropped into the water below, and disappeared, and Pen, as he rode home that night, actually thought about someone but himself.

W. G. HOSKINS

The Big House
and
the Squire

W. G. Hoskins, Exeter-born and educated, was Reader in
Economic History at Oxford, and is Emeritus Professor of
English History (University of Leicester). His many works on
regional history are definitive: this extract is from *Devon* (1954).

The social revolution in the Devonshire countryside takes much
the same form as elsewhere in rural England. The atmosphere of
slow decay about the country houses is perhaps a little more
noticeable, for so much of Devonshire society centred round the
squire, and there are so many of these houses. What has happened
to the big houses of a hundred years ago? If we look back to the
largest houses and estates of 1850 and see how they fare today,
what sort of picture do we get? The enormous Rolle estate is
merged with that of Lord Clinton (who is now probably the
largest landowner in Devon), and the Rolles' house of Stevenstone
is an ugly ruin in a naked and devastated park. The Courtenays
will still keep up Powderham, but every few years see more sales
of their land. The Aclands live in a corner of Killerton, and have
given a great part of their estate to the National Trust. Most of
Killerton now serves as a workers' holiday centre.

The earls and dukes of Bedford never had a mansion in Devon. They had a town house in Exeter (gone long ago) and a 'cottage' at Endsleigh, deep in a park of some 3,400 acres above the wooded Tamar valley, which is still used by the family for fishing holidays.

The Bampfyldes' house at Poltimore is now a private hospital. The Earls of Portsmouth have left Eggesford (only built in 1832) to fall into ruin; the Carews have abandoned Haccombe in recent years; the Lopes (Lord Roborough) have gone from Maristow, which is now a home for aged clergy. Tawstock, once the home of the Earls of Bath, is a school. Only three great houses are still occupied by their old owners—Powderham, Saltram, and Castle Hill. This is the fate, then, of the ten largest houses and estates of 1850.

Of the squires' houses, the same melancholy tale can be told. Only two or three are occupied by ancient families: the Fulfords continue at Great Fulford, the Cruwys at Cruwys Morchard. But Kelly is a hotel, and so, too, is Portledge, the home of the Coffins since the 12th century. Bradfield, home of the Walronds since the time of John, is a public institution. Dartington and Tapeley are schools. The mighty tribe of Chichester, who once ramified over North Devon in ten or a dozen branches, are now narrowed down to Hall, in Bishop's Tawton.

But what atmosphere there is in these old homes where they are still lived in! The past is alive in every corner of them, in every piece of furniture, every turn in the stairs and every window-seat. They are

> Thronged with quiet, inoffensive ghosts,
> Impalpable impressions on the air—
> A sense of something moving to and fro.

There is the small collection of paintings up the staircase, mostly of the eighteenth century, pedestrian portraits of Georgian squires with hand tucked in ample, silken waistcoat, and their pudding-faced ladies; generally one attributed hesitantly and modestly to Gainsborough, but most of them, one suspects, done by painters like William Gandy on an off day.

In the library, looking out over the weed-enamelled drive and a park still timbered with walnut and oak and beech, the Victorian bookshelves rise to the ceiling and hold copies of Ovid and Horace used at Oxford by Georgian ancestors; dark, calf-bound, the faint, spidery brown handwriting. On the bottom shelves is an early edition of the *Encyclopaedia Britannica* (an edition published before the Age of Steam but still occasionally useful). Somewhere nearer at hand is an old edition of Burn's *Justice of the Peace and Parish Officer*, perhaps an early run of the *Railway Magazine*, and row upon row of unreadable sermons, old botany books, bird books, fishing books, parish histories, the proceedings of the local antiquarian society of forty years ago, and a whole shelf on gardening. Papers cascade out of writing-desks as old as the room; dogs snuffle quietly in Queen Anne wing-chairs; photographs of cricket elevens may be observed in obscure corners close to the stuffed corncrake, of Harrow, Winchester, and Eton long ago.

In the billiard-room, still occasionally used, are the nondescript paintings seconded to its walls about the year 1870 and since forgotten, and the assegais sent home from the Zulu wars by some great-uncle. And outside is the high-walled garden, warm in the sun, with its deep black earth spade-turned century after century; and the turret over the hall roof, with its silent bell. And just beyond the garden, among the tree-tops, one sees the pinnacles of the parish church, and one hears the clock striking the hours, day after day, season after season, for ever and ever, as they once thought. Here, where all is quiet, the lunacy of the outside world, the fate that has overtaken it, is an insoluble mystery. One ruminates over it for a few minutes after the nine o'clock news, heard religiously each evening in the library on an antique and sizzling battery set. With relief the squire turns to the local newspaper, produced in the market town a dozen miles away, and reads the more intelligible and interesting news about the doings of his own countryside.*

In the parish church the squire still sits in his own pew, with perhaps only three or four other people in the Sunday morning congregation. The service is simple and Protestant, in accord with the decent box-pews and the neat pulpit. In the chancel, or above the family pew, are the marble and brass memorials to his more recent ancestors—soldiers nearly all of them—com-

---

*The above description is a composite one. No particular house is intended, but every detail is authentic.

memorating every obscure war that Britain fought during the 19th century on far-away frontiers. Saddest of all are the memorials of the First World War.

The year 1914 marked the end of an age, the end of the country house, and the squire, and the old village life. So many of the sons and heirs of the old estates, following the traditions of their families, led those futile, hopeless attacks through the mud of northern France and Flanders, and fell there. One often reflects, looking at these plain, unassuming tablets on the chancel wall, or in some family chapel in the now deserted aisle, that the year 1916 above all gave the real death-blow to the country houses: when, on that terrible river the Somme, on that far-away July morning with the larks singing above the battlefield, so many young officers perished, leading their men. The Somme is com-memorated on English chancel walls everywhere; and on the village greens, too, one reads the names of the men who followed, and perished likewise in that distant summer. At Upton Pyne, in the empty sunlight, where hardly a young man is to be seen today, the cross outside the churchyard gate records the names of sixteen men killed from this small parish alone. Hardly a family escaped. And so it was, to a greater or lesser degree, in every village. That year, and the two years that followed, did much to put an end to the traditional village life, the counterpart to the life at the great house, when the young men who would have carried on the trades and traditions of their fathers, and would have been the fathers of the next generation, failed to return. And now the tablets are going up for yet another war, mercifully with far fewer names on them, but often the same family names as those of the earlier years.

Nearly all the squires have gone. Even if the family has not died out, it has vacated the big house and usually left the parish to live elsewhere. No one has taken the place of the squire. The smaller houses—the houses of the 'squireens'—fall empty, too. Their old owners go, but these houses are quickly filled by retired military and naval officers (mostly the former) who buy them shorn of most of their land and treat them sympathetically. Occasionally one sees unfortunate and tasteless 'modernisation', but it is rare. One can generally assume that wherever one sees a good Georgian or older house in a little paddock it is occupied

by a colonel or a brigadier. The Devonshire countryside is thick
with army men, who do not, however, and cannot, take the place
of the squire. Here the vacuum remains.

DYLAN THOMAS

The Crumbs of One Man's Year

Dylan Thomas (1914–53), most individual of Welsh poets, broadcast 'The Crumbs of One Man's Year' in the BBC Home Service, December 1946. Aneirin Talfan Davies, of the Welsh Region, BBC, who edited *Quite Early One Morning* (1954) in which the talk appeared posthumously, praised 'the deliberate skill of the craftsman who weighed every word and every syllable'.

Thomas knew the West Country. Indeed, he was married there —in the Registrar's Office at Penzance on 11 June, 1937. He and Caitlin Macnamara had gone down to Mousehole in the late spring and they remained all that summer in West Cornwall.

Slung as though in a hammock, or a lull, between one Christmas for ever over and a New Year nearing full of relentless surprises, waywardly and gladly I pry back at these wizening twelve months and see only a waltzing snippet of the tipsy-turvy times, flickers of vistas, flashes of queer fishes, patches and chequers of a bard's-eye view.

Of what is coming in the New Year I know nothing, except that all that is certain will come like thunderclaps or like comets in the shape of four-leaved clovers, and that all that is unforeseen will appear with the certainty of the sun who every morning shakes a leg in the sky; and of what has gone I know only shilly-shally snatches and freckled plaids, flecks and dabs, dazzle and froth; a simple second caught in coursing snow-light, an instant, gay or sorry, struck motionless in the curve of flight like a bird or a scythe; the spindrift leaf and stray-paper whirl, canter, quarrel, and people-chase of everybody's street; suddenly the way the grotesque wind slashes and freezes at a corner the clothes of a passer-by so that she stays remembered, cold and still until the world like a night-light in a nursery goes out; and a waddling couple of the small occurrences, comic as ducks, that quack their way through our calamitous days; whits and dots and tittles.

'Look back, back,' the big voices clarion, 'look back at the black colossal year,' while the rich music fanfares and dead-marches.

I can give you only a scattering of some of the crumbs of one man's year; and the penny music whistles.

Any memory, of the long, revolving year, will do, to begin with.

I was walking, one afternoon in August, along a river-bank, thinking the same thoughts that I always think when I walk along a river-bank in August. As I was walking, I was thinking—now it is August and I am walking along a river-bank. I do not think I was thinking of anything else. I should have been thinking of what I should have been doing, but I was thinking only of what I was doing then and it was all right: it was good, and ordinary, and slow, and idle, and old, and sure, and what I was doing I could have been doing a thousand years before, had I been alive then and myself or any other man. You could have thought the river was ringing—almost you could hear the green, rapid bells sing in it: it could have been the River Elusina, 'that dances at the noise of Musick, for with Musick it bubbles, dances and growes sandy, and so continues till the musick ceases . . .' or it could have been the river 'in Judea that runs swiftly all the six dayes of the week, and stands still and rests all their Sabbath'. There were trees blowing, standing still, growing, knowing, whose names I never knew. (Once, indeed, with a friend I wrote a poem beginning, 'All trees are oaks, except fir-trees.') There were birds being busy, or sleep-flying, in the sky. (The poem

had continued: 'All birds are robins, except crows, or rooks.')
Nature was doing what it was doing, and thinking just that.
And I was walking and thinking that I was walking, and for
August it was not such a cold day. And then I saw, drifting along
the water, a piece of paper, and I thought: Something wonderful
may be written on this paper. I was alone on the gooseberry
earth, or alone for two green miles, and a message drifted towards
me on that tabby-coloured water that ran through the middle of
the cow-patched, mooing fields. It was a message from multi-
tudinous nowhere to my solitary self. I put out my stick and
caught the piece of paper and held it close to the river-bank. It
was a page torn from a very old periodical. That I could see.
I leant over and read, through water, the message on the rippling
page. I made out, with difficulty, only one sentence: it commemor-
ated the fact that, over a hundred years ago, a man in Worcester
had, for a bet, eaten, at one sitting, fifty-two pounds of plums.

And any other memory, of the long evolving year, will do,
to go on with.

Here now, to my memory, come peaceful blitz and pieces of
the Fifth of November, guys in the streets and forks in the sky,
when Catherine-wheels and Jacky-jumps and good bombs burst in
the blistered areas. The rockets are few but they star between
roofs and up to the wall of the warless night. 'A penny for the
Guy?' 'No, that's my father.' The great joke brocks and sizzles.
Sirius explodes in the backyard by the shelter. Timorous ladies
sit in their back-rooms, with the eighth programme on very loud.
Retiring men snarl under their blankets. In the unkempt-gardens
of the very rich, the second butler lights a squib. In everybody's
street the fearless children shout, under the little, homely raids. But
I was standing on a signalling country hill where they fed a
hungry bonfire Guy with brushwood, sticks, and cracker-jacks;
the bonfire Guy whooped for more; small sulphurous puddings
banged in his burning belly, and his thorned hair caught. He
lurched and made common noises. He was a long time dying on
the hill over the starlit fields where the tabby river, without a
message, ran on, with bells and trout and tins and bangles and
literature and cats in it, to the sea never out of sound.

And on one occasion, in this long dissolving year, I remember
that I boarded a London bus from a district I have forgotten,

and where I certainly could have been up to little good, to an appointment that I did not want to keep.

It was a shooting green spring morning, nimble and crocus, with all the young women treading on naked flower-stalks, the metropolitan sward, swinging their milk-pail handbags, gentle, fickle, inviting, accessible, forgiving each robustly abandoned gesture of salutation before it was made or imagined, assenting, as they revelled demurely towards the manicure *salon* or the type-writing office, to all the ardent unspoken endearments of shaggy strangers and the winks and pipes of clovenfooted sandwichmen. The sun shrilled, the buses gambolled, policemen and daffodils bowed in the breeze that tasted of buttermilk. Delicate carousal plashed and babbled from the public-houses which were not yet open. I felt like a young god. I removed my collar-studs and opened my shirt. I tossed back my hair. There was an aviary in my heart, but without any owls or eagles. My cheeks were cherried warm. I smelt, I thought, of sea-pinks. To the sound of madrigals sung by slim sopranos in waterfalled valleys where I was the only tenor, I leapt on to a bus. The bus was full. Carefree, open-collared, my eyes alight, my veins full of the spring as a dancer's shoes should be full of champagne, I stood, in love and at ease and always young, on the packed lower deck. And a man of exactly my own age—or perhaps he was a little older—got up and offered me his seat. He said, in a respectful voice, as though to an old justice of the peace, 'Please, won't you take my seat?' and then he added—'Sir.'

How many variegations of inconsiderable defeats and disillusionments I have forgotten! How many shades and shapes from the polychromatic zebra house! How many Joseph-coats I have left uncalled-for in the Gentlemen's Cloakrooms of the year!

And one man's year is like the country of a cloud, mapped on the sky, that soon will vanish into the watery, ordered wastes, into the spinning rule, into the dark which is light. Now the cloud is flying, very slowly, out of sight, and I can remember of all that voyaging geography, no palaced morning hills or huge plush valleys in the downing sun, forests simmering with birds, stagged moors, merry legendary meadowland, bullish plains, but only— the street near Waterloo station where a small boy, wearing cut-down khaki and a steel helmet, pushed a pram full of firewood and shouted, in a dispassionate voice, after each passer-by: 'Where's your tail?'

The estuary pool under the collapsed castle, where the July children rolled together in original mud, shrieking and yawping, and low life, long before newts twitched on their hands.

The crisp path through the field in this December snow, in the deep dark, where we trod the buried grass like ghosts on dry toast.

The single-line run along the spring-green river-bank where water voles went Indian file to work, and where the young impatient voles, in their sleek vests, always in a hurry, jumped over the threadbare backs of the old ones.

The razor-scarred back-street café bar where a man with cut cheeks and chewed ears, huskily and furiously complained, over tarry tea, that the new baby panda in the zoo was not floodlit.

The gully sands in March, under the flayed and flailing cliff-top trees, when the wind played old Harry, or old Thomas, with me, and cormorants, far off, sped like motor-boats across the bay, as I weaved towards the toppling town and the black, loud *Lion* where the cat, who purred like a fire, looked out of two cinders at the gently swilling retired sea-captains in the snug-as-a-bug back bar.

And the basement kitchen in nipping February, with napkins on the line swung across from door to chockablock corner, and a bicycle by the larder very much down at wheels, and hats and toy-engines and bottles and spanners on the broken rocking- chair, and billowing papers and half-finished crosswords stacked on the radio always turned full tilt, and the fire smoking, and onions peeling, and chips always spitting on the stove, and small men in their overcoats talking of self-discipline and the ascetic life until the air grew woodbine-blue and the clock choked and the traffic died.

And then the moment of a night in that cavorting spring, rare and unforgettable as a bicycle-clip found in the middle of the desert. The lane was long and soused and dark that led to the house I helped to fill and bedraggle.

'Who's left this in this corner?'

'What where?'

'Here this.'

A doll's arm, the chitterlings of a clock, a saucepan full of hatbands.

The lane was rutted as though by bosky watercarts, and so dark you couldn't see your front in spite of you. Rain barrelled down. On one side you couldn't hear the deer that lived there, and on the other side—voices began to whisper, muffled in the midnight sack. A man's voice and a woman's voice. 'Lovers,' I said to myself. For at night the heart comes out, like a cat on the tiles. Discourteously I shone my torch. There, in the thick rain, a young man and a young woman stood, very close together, near the hedge that whirred in the wind. And a yard from them, another young man sat staidly, on the grass verge, holding an open book from which he appeared to read. And in the very rutted and puddly middle of the lane, two dogs were fighting, with brutish concentration and in absolute silence.

DEREK TANGYE

Towards Minack

Derek Tangye, a distinguished Fleet Street writer and a Cornish-man whose ancestors had come from Brittany at the beginning of the fifteenth century, decided with his wife Jeannie to leave London 'in favour of the bathless, paraffin-lit two-roomed cottage called Minack, and six acres of uncultivated land on the coast between Penzance and Land's End'.

'Our livelihood,' he wrote, 'now depended upon the creation of a flower farm from this desolate, beautiful country, aided not by any practical experience, but only by our ignorance as to what lay ahead.'

In *A Gull on the Roof* (1961), first of a long sequence of successful books, he described how Minack was found.

We had been playing the game of looking for somewhere to settle whenever we had taken our holidays in Cornwall. We wanted a cottage with a wood near by and fields that went down to the sea, distant from any other habitation and remote from a countrified imitation of the life we were wishing to leave. Some-where where we could earn a living and yet relish the isolation of a South Sea island, be able to think without being told what to think, to have the leisure to study the past, to live the present without interference.

It is a game which is perfectly harmless so long as no place you see fits your ideal. Once the two coincide the moment of decision arrives and it is no longer a game. This is what happened when Jeannie and I found Minack.

We had set out one May morning, from the inn in the Valley of Lamorna, to walk westwards along the coast. We were on a week's holiday and as usual the carrot dangling before us on the walk was our imaginary home.

Lamorna was once the centre of quarrying and its beauty was incidental. The great blocks of granite were blasted from the cliff face beside the little harbour, transported in long wooden wagons pulled by teams of horses up and down the hills to Penzance where they were cut into the required shapes and shipped for building purposes all over Britain.

The name means valley by the sea, and it is now a sleepy wooded valley possessing the ethereal beauty, the lush vegetation and shimmering colours, the away from it all atmosphere which tempts people to believe that here is their earthly Nirvana. In the summer, of course, it erupts with a lava of holidaymakers yet, and this is the charm of Lamorna, there is no strident attempt to exploit these visitors. There is the inn, a small hotel, Ernie Walter's filling station and cafe, Daniel's place down in the Cove; and though a few cottages advertise bed and breakfast in their windows, one feels this is done out of courtesy rather than a desire to earn a living. Lamorna, then, is a pilgrimage of the day tripper and though the narrow road on a summer afternoon is choked with cars, charabancs and dust, the evening comes and the valley is silent again. In winter it is always silent except for the wind in the trees and the echo of the surf in the cove, and it becomes a valley to cure a cynic. The air is sweet with the scent of the violet plants which climb up the hillside in neat cultivated rows, and as you walk along you will meet a picker, a basket of violets or anemones in either hand, taking them home to bunch. Or in the early spring when cities are still shivering, you will find the valley a factory of flowers with every inhabitant a picker or a buncher, sharing in the hectic race to harvest the daffodils before those 'up along' come into bloom. During the war growers had to surrender a large part of their daffodil ground to the growing of vegetables, and so they threw their bulbs at random in the woods. The effect in the spring is as if the constellations had left their places in the sky for Lamorna woods, a myriad yellow lights peeping from the undergrowth, edging the sparkling stream beside moss-covered boulders, struggling through twining, unfriendly brambles.

The path we walked along was only the shadow of a path, more like the trodden run of badgers. Here, because there was no sign of habitation, because the land and the boulders and the rocks embraced the sea without interference, we could sense we were part of the beginning of time, the centuries of unceasing waves, the unseen pattern of the wild generations of foxes and badgers, the ageless gales that had lashed the desolate land, exultant and roaring, a giant harbour of sunken ships in their wake. And we came to a point, after a steep climb, where a great Carn stood balanced on a smaller one, upright like a huge man standing on a stool, as if it were a sentinel waiting to hail the ghosts of lost sailors. The track, on the other side, had tired of the undergrowth which blocked its way along the head of the cliff, for it sheered seawards tumbling in a zigzag course to the scarred grey rocks below. We stood on the pinnacle ... the curve of Mount's Bay leading to the Lizard Point on the left, the Wolf Rock lighthouse a speck in the distance, a French crabber a mile off-shore, pale blue hull and small green sail aft, chugging through the white speckled sea towards Newlyn, and high above us a buzzard, its wings spread motionless, soaring effortlessly into the sky.

Jeannie suddenly pointed inland. 'Look!' she said, 'there it is!'

There was never any doubt in either of our minds. The small grey cottage a mile away, squat in the lonely landscape, surrounded by trees and edged into the side of a hill, became as if by magic the present and the future. It was as if a magician beside this ancient Carn had cast a spell upon us, so that we could touch the future as we could, at that moment, touch the Carn. There in the distance we could see our figures moving about our daily tasks, a thousand, thousand figures criss-crossing the untamed land, dissolving into each other, leaving a mist of excitement of our times to come.

We stood outside the cottage and stared; a Hans Andersen cottage with the primitive beauty of a crofter's home, sad and neglected as if it were one of the grey boulders in the white land around. The walls seemed to grow out of the ground, great rocks fingering up the sides until they met the man-placed stones, rough-faced granite slabs bound together by clay. Once upon a time, it appeared to us, there might have been upstairs rooms and perhaps a roof of thatch; but now the roof was an uncouth corrugated iron jagged with holes, tilting so steeply that it resembled a man's cap pulled over his eyes; and prodding defiantly into the sky above it, as if ashamed of being associated with such ugliness, was a massive lichen-covered chimney. The poky windows peered from the darkness within, three facing the moorland and the sea, and two either side of the battered door which looked upon the unkempt once loved tiny garden. We pushed the door and it was unlocked. Wooden boards peppered with holes gnawed by rats covered the floor, and putting my hand through one of them I touched the wet earth. The walls were mustard yellow with old paper and though the area of the cottage was that of an old-fashioned drawing-room it was divided into four rooms, matchbox thick divisions yielding the effect of privacy. At right angles to the door in a cavity of the wall beneath the chimney, an ancient Cornish range seared with rust, droppings of rats dirtying the oven, brandished the memories of forgotten meals. Above, the sagging thin boards of the ceiling dropped in curves, rimmed grey in patches from rain dripping through the roof. A cupboard faced the door and inside broken crockery lay on the shelves, a brown kettle without a lid, and a mug imprinted with a coloured picture of King George V and Queen Mary side by side. Musty with long absence of an inhabitant, lugubrious with the crush of the toy-sized rooms, the cottage seemed yet to shine with welcome; and we felt as if we had entered Aladdin's Cave.

Outside we stood by the corner of the cottage, the battered door facing climbing ground behind us, and looked down upon a shadow of a valley, gentle slopes, heading for the sea. Beyond was the Carn where we had stood, cascading below it a formation of rocks resembling an ancient castle, and in the distance across the blue carpet of sea the thin white line of breakers dashing against the shores of Prah Sands, Porthleven, and Mullion. A lane drifted away from the cottage. On its right was a barn with feet-thick walls in which were open slits instead of windows and on its left was a tumbled down stone hedge, holding back the woods we had seen and the jungle-like growth, as policemen try to hold back a bursting throng. The lane led down to a stream, dammed into a pool by the density of the weeds which blocked the outflow, and then, a few yards on, petered out in a tangle of brushwood and gorse bushes. We could see that the cottage was only connected with civilisation by a track through a field.

There was another track which led towards the sea and, as it broke away from the environment of the cottage, we found roofless outbuildings, bramble covered stone walls, with black-thorn growing where once stood men and cattle sheltering from the weather. The track broke into a huge field or what we could see by the hedges was once a field but now had grown into part of the desolate moorland, then fell downwards to the top of the cliff. It was no ordinary cliff. It did not fall fearsomely sheer to the sea below but dropped a jungle of thorns, gorse, elderberry trees and waist-high couch grass, in a series of leaps to a rugged teaspoon of a bay; and as we stood there, somnolent gulls sitting on the rocks far below, we saw in our minds a giant knife slicing pocket meadows out of the rampaging vegetation, refashioning the cliff so that it resembled the neat pattern of daffodil and potato gardens that were grouped like hillside Italian vineyards at intervals along the coast. We saw in our minds not only a way of life, but also the means by which to earn a living. It was the sweet moment when the wings of enthusiasm take flight, when victory is untarnished by endeavour, the intoxicating instant when the urge for conquest obliterates the reallty of obstacles, dissolving common sense, blanketing the possibility of failure. We had found our imaginary home. If we were able to possess it the way stretched clear to our contentment.

Details about the cottage were told to us back at the inn. Mrs Emily Bailey, who was then the innkeeper, and Tom her son who nursed the adjoining market garden but who now had taken her place—these two listened patiently to our excitement. It was the habit of holidaymakers to lean over the bar expounding their hopes of packing up jobs, seeking an answer as to where they could escape; and these words of good intentions were as familiar to Tom and Mrs Bailey as the good-byes at the end of holidays, a part of the holiday as splits and Cornish cream, a game of make-believe that was played for a fortnight, then forgotten for another year.

The cottage was on the land of a farm which belonged to one of the great Cornish estates. This Estate rented the farm to a large farmer who lived a few miles from Land's End who, in turn, sublet it out on a dairyman's lease. This lease was a relic of those days when Estates had difficulty in finding tenants for their farms. An established farmer would rent an unwanted farm, stock it with cattle and hire out each cow to a man of his own choosing who would occupy the farmhouse and farm the land. Hence this man, or dairyman as he was called, had no responsibility to the Estate for he was only a cowman. The responsibility of upkeep lay in the hands of the absentee farmer . . .

[After meeting the farmer next day, and a six months' interval, the Tangyes were told that they could live at Minack. Their first visit to the cottage, with their cat Monty, was during a weekend in November.]

It was nearly midnight, on that first visit, when the three of us reached Penzance. A gale was blowing in from the sea and as we drove along the front cascades of spray drenched the car as if coming from a giant hose. We crossed Newlyn Bridge, then up steep Paul Hill and along the winding road past the turn to Lamorna Valley; then up another hill, Boleigh Hill, where King Athelstan fought the Cornish ten centuries ago. Rain was whipping the windscreen when we turned off the road along a lane, through the dark shadows of a farm, until it petered out close to the cliff's edge. I got out and opened a gate, then drove bumpily across a field with the headlights swathing a way through a carpet of escaping rabbits. This, the back entrance to Minack, was the way we had to use until the bramble covered lane was opened up again; and after I pulled up beside a stone hedge, we still had two fields to scramble across in the darkness and the rain and the gale before we reached the cottage.

I lit a candle, and the light quivered on the peeling, yellow papered walls. Everything was the same as the day we first pushed open the door; the ancient Cornish range, the pint-sized rooms with their matchbox thick divisions, the wooden floor peppered with holes—only it was raining now and above the howl of the gale was the steady drip, drip of water from the leaking roof.

We didn't care. The adventure had begun.

J. C. TREWIN

South

Notes for the first chapter of a revised autobiography.

I

Gwinear Road—Praze ('Hallelujah!' added the porter, merry man) —Nancegollan—Truthall (a platform merely)—then Helston and rail's end. For all we knew on this night in 1917, the branch train, dawdling moodily to the buffers, could have been stiff after its burial in the Great Blizzard of '91, a frolic few away from the West could remember. But we had jarred to a halt. Out quickly now, under the oil lamps that burned a smoky primrose, through the station yard warm with voices, and into the jingle, or pony-trap, where our driver waited to flick his whip and send us swinging into the dark. Helston, metropolis of Meneage, with its tilted cross of lights, and the gurgle and lapse of water in the street runnels, dimmed behind us. We were heading due south, out by Culdrose meadows (lost today under the great naval air station) where long ago my grandfather had farmed; then along the last grey ribbon of Cornish road that spanned the all-but-island of the Lizard peninsula. At its end there would be a simple choice. We could stay, return as we had come, or take a high dive into the foam, somewhere round Maenheere and the Stags. To be 'stagged' is to be trapped; the Lizard reefs have bitterly deserved their name.

We could feel a nip in the spring night. At Cury Cross Lanes a sneaping wind whistled from the east, above the acres of Goon-hilly, the Wisht Land ('the wylde morre, called Gunhilly'), over Leech Pool and Dry Tree (site of the gibbet), furze and stone, heather and tumuli, the dark, shorn barrens of the south. Presently we were under the boughs in the sudden vale of Bochym; up again—conscious of that hidden, distant sea on three sides of us— and trotting mile by mile across the plateau until a sparse twinkle of windows showed immediately ahead: the lights of Lizard Town. On now towards the village, by-passing the church-town of Landewednack. We twisted past the 'Free Church' (United Methodist chapel) and quiet Green; dipped to a straggle of cottages and a final serpentine-turner's shed (a glow within, and the churring of the wheel); climbed once more, and then, sharply right, the salt air lapping us, towards the red, rubbed gates beyond Pen-menner. Here were the fuchsias' sway, the soft feathering of the tamarisks, and in a moment lamplight filling an open door. Before us, and darkened now, lawn, kitchen-garden, and barley-field fell to Old Lizard Head and, somewhere beyond it, Brazil. About us we heard the tide's incessant wash and drag. This was way down south, eleven miles past Helston, and (though I would not have put it like that), the tip of an Elizabethan stage thrust out into the southern sea. Plymouth, and my new school, were in another planet, an infinite distance up the Great Western rail, over the divide of the Tamar, and, before this, Brunel only knew how many viaducts and high-flung bridges across the stretched spine of Cornwall.

Only my mother and second sister would be at home. My elder sister, in this war of which I knew little, was a VAD at Exeter. My father, a merchant captain and a deep-water sailor if ever there was one, was away, leading an Atlantic convoy. One of a family of seamen traceable to the sixteenth century, he had been bred in the East Cornish fishing hamlet of Gorran Haven which in his youth appeared to be as remote and independent as Andorra, though I gathered that there was a working arrangement with the county of Cornwall, and, through this, with the Empire beyond. Cornish of the Cornish—the name means a white homestead—he never ceased to be angry at any mispronunciation: 'Get it right!... Say Tremayne, Trelawny, Trewin.' Still, it could have been worse: he might have been called (as his mother had been) Tregidgo.

My own mother's name was much easier. She was a James (with Rowes, Courtenays and Hockings in her ancestry), and she came, fifth of seven children—six sisters and a brother—from St Anthony-in-Meneage; a farmhouse in the coil of lanes above

the oak-shelved, heron-haunted shores of Helford river. Long
before I was born she had spent most of her time sailing with
Father, anywhere, it seemed, between Iquique, Rosario, or
Zonguldak. She told me, after consideration, that she had seldom
had more time for sewing.

She would have been at it on the morning after I came home;
sitting calmly in the window that looked across to Kynance Cove.
Meanwhile, according to first-day ritual, I was hurrying to the sea,
down Rocky Lane, a tumbled rabbit-drive, sunk in its matted
fern-growth between bramble and boulder; at its foot the hummocked pasture of Pistol Meadow, heavy with the tang of seaweed
and camomile. Probably its name derived from the Cornish
word for a stream that ran through to gush over the cliff: but
enduring local tradition remembered a disaster in the first half
of the eighteenth century. Then a transport with seven hundred
men dashed itself to wreck on Maenheere (or Man o' War) reef;
two hundred bodies were buried in pits upon the cliff-top, and
so many fire-arms were picked up that the place became known as
Pistol. I could believe anything of this eerie, mounded field lifted
above the cove, a rug of mesembryanthemum ('sally-me-'ansome')
knotted upon the verge, and a descent to the beach by a steeply-
trenched gully. This was no more than a chute with primitive,
broken steps, a corroded rail on one side of it, and before long, on
the other side, a sheer drop. I knew most of Pistol's crevices, its
limpet-plated rocks, the natural arch, the baulks of water-weighted
driftwood, and the solitaire-marble pebbles cluttered beneath the
steps. Yet, though I went there often, at all hours of the day and
months of the year, I was rarely at ease, sometimes scrambling
away up the stair and across the meadow as though every fiend was
following. Memories have lingered through life:

> I call my name, and I answer
>   Far down in the cove,
> But I stand by the mounds in the meadow above.

> . Here the camomile-breath is harsh by the brook,
>   And down there below
> It's only the brine and the weed that I know.

Down, down, round the rock-pools
  A boy cannot dread
The cold day in the meadow when childhood is dead.

It's that day in the meadow,
  And lost up above
I cry to my old life far down in the cove.

II

After Pistol, on that first morning home, I would have raced up to
Old Lizard Head which some facetious Victorian christened Lord
Brougham's Nose—not that many people would search for a
likeness in the weathered profile. For me this was (and remains)
England's south, even though the Ordnance Survey believes in a
suavely-sliding promontory between Polpeor and Housel, far less
dramatic than the height of Old Lizard with its gull's-eye view
of the last of England; westward, far across the water, is the dark
and rival peninsula of Penwith, a sinister coast, Land's End. Old
Lizard calls for ceremony. There used to be on it (possibly still is)
a coastguard's notched look-out pole. Having read a purplish
passage in Bulwer Lytton's *Leila*, beginning 'To Boabdil el Chico,
King of Granada, Ferdinand of Aragon and Isabel of Castile
send royal greeting', I would frequently address the pole, sending it
royal greeting and offering princely territories in the Alpuxarras
mountains to its sway.

The headland is unchanged. So, farther on, beyond Caerthillian,
is the broad scarf of Pentreath where, at low evening tide, one
could go launcing in the moonlight: not a country dance but the
pursuit of a tiny, silver-streaking sand-eel: an exercise once recorded
by a Lizard artist, Sydney Hart. Farther yet are the elaborations of
Kynance Cove, moulded and colour-veined in serpentine, the
Gull Rock, the Steeple and Asparagus Island, the Lion massively
on its haunches: all disposed by an expert director, not to mask
each other. Kynance, with the Rill Head (from which the crescent
moon of the Spanish Armada was sighted on a July evening in
1588) was the first picture I saw every morning on waking in my
attic. I remember, too—when about five—jumping from bed
late on a summer night (late to me; possibly eleven o'clock or so),

hearing distant laughter, and running to the window to watch points of fire that glittered and flitted above Caerthillian. The ray of the Lizard lighthouse, from behind me, swung across the dark. The gleaming points vanished, returned, vanished. For five minutes I stood there, staring at the moon, the stroke of the skimming beam from the east, and the odd sparkling fires that leapt and shone. These, I heard next day, were visitors going home along the cliffs with driftwood torches. It was twenty-five years before I discovered a phrase, in a letter of Thomas Lovell Beddoes on the fireflies of Milan, that described for me what I had seen that night: 'Their bright light is evanescent, and alternates with the darkness as if the swift wheeling of the earth struck fire out of the black atmosphere; as if the winds were being set upon the planetary grindstone and gave out such momentary sparks from their edges.'

Kynance, tough going for an eight-year-old, would have been my limit on the first morning back. Next day I would have run through the inland straggle of Lizard Town, across the endeared but messy Green with its serpentine-workers' huts, and on over the ruler-straight Beacon. On the left, before the school, was the Reading Room, probably the most versatile hall on the Lizard peninsula. Everything happened there, flower shows, bazaars, political meetings (few of these), concerts, any sort of village assembly, even some early films. One night, in *Uncle Tom's Cabin*, Little Eva died upside down after a very long wait for the film to begin. News went round that the limelight was 'scat', which sounded like a highly technical and proper reason, and was repeated with much head-shaking.

Wearing prickly epaulettes, I took part, as Nelson, in a Mrs Jarley's waxwork show, though respect for history does make me wonder whether this might not have been in the schoolroom next door. Certainly it was there that I recited, at speed and to a rataplan of rain on the windows, several stanzas from 'The Lay of Lake Regillus', most of the proper names murdered. (I had been pardoned long before my next appearance years later when I presented the school prizes in the Reading Room.) Any dramatic scenes were rare: we could have the novelty of films, but flesh-and-blood acting—work of the 'pomping folk'—was not well regarded. It was a decade or so before I knew that Henry Irving (Johnnie

Brodribb), Somerset-born but with a Cornish mother, had been brought up during the 1840s at Halsetown behind St Ives—about nineteen miles from us. We hear of the haunted quality of Irving's performances; I wonder now and then whether they might not have gained something from the influence of that still strange and haunted back of beyond. It took me even longer to realise that in 1880 Forbes-Robertson and Helena Modjeska, pomping folk on holiday, had acted the Balcony Scene from *Romeo and Juliet* in Ruan Minor only two miles off; they played by moonlight, using a platform run up by coastguards in the rectory garden before high elms.

We were not Shakespearians at The Lizard; so he had to be discovered. For this I thank the shade of the nineteenth century historical novelist, Harrison Ainsworth. His books may not be much read now, but I remember two in particular: *The Tower of London*, which begins with a sentence of 262 words; and *Old St Paul's*, which I enjoyed even more—reasonably, because Ainsworth is describing the Plague and the Fire and has a hero who cries 'in an impassioned tone', 'Do not fly me, Amabel, but suffer me to declare the love I have for you'. She does, and he 'imprints a kiss on her snowy brow'. There is also a villain who is stifled, with his partner in iniquity, when a splendid cascade of molten lead floods the vaults under blazing St Paul's.

You will understand, as the Victorian punster said, that with all their vaults I enjoyed the books immensely. My father, who also appreciated Ainsworth, took with him on every voyage a fresh collection of books, the weirdest mixture—*The Stones of Venice*, *What Katy Did*, Morley's *Life of Gladstone*—and left the old ones behind him. Being often alone, I read everything that was handy. This was why Ainsworth brought me to Shakespeare. I have heard a suggestion that the book could have been Lew Wallace's *Ben-Hur* (with the chariot-race) which was also in a green binding; but I think now it was *Old St Paul's*. Anyway, one fierce evening in winter, I stood on tip-toe in front of the fire to pull Ainsworth from an upper shelf and get back to the cascade of molten lead. The books were a tight fit. Instead, I pulled down a large volume of Shakespeare, something I had never tried before; it fell on the rug, an enormous bearskin, in front of the hearth, and there and

then I settled to read it at the page where it had opened. This was
at the beginning of one of the last plays I would meet in the theatre,
the First Part of *Henry VI*, and at the lines (Henry V's funeral)
where the Duke of Bedford, apostrophising largely, cries:

> Comets, importing change of times and states,
> Brandish your crystal tresses in the sky . . .

It seemed to me a precise description of the flash of the Lizard
Light. Obviously the plays were worthwhile and I continued with
them, going inevitably to the wrong ones first. My Shakespeare
was a snobbish affair that segregated the non-Folio *Pericles* at the
back, beyond the Poems. Naturally, I started with this and made
uncommonly little of it—except the scene when Diana appears to
the sleeping Pericles. I thought his cry to her, 'Celestial Dian,
goddess argentine!' was the most exciting thing I had known, and
I ran round the village addressing it to the least likely people who
said simply, 'The boy's mazed!' and walked on. It would be a
quarter of a century before *Pericles* turned up in the theatre. I was
still excited.

III

We should be still on the Beacon, by the Reading Room and
school. Swiftly forward now, past the Wesleyan chapel where
we sang on winter nights 'Glorious things of Thee are spoken,
Zion, city of Our God', and downhill to the church-town of
Landewednack in the bosom of the trees. There the church stood
with its chequered granite and serpentine tower, the zig-zags of its
Norman doorway, and the underwater light within. Church Cove,
at the foot of a sharp descent, was once a day's march from home.
I might get home (very late) by the path from the Cove that clung
to every seam and inlet of the cliffs, round Bass Point and Penolver.
At one point it fell to the ravine of Housel Bay, the exclamation
mark of the Bumble Rock, and the tilted cavity of Lion's Den, then
climbed again to the lime-washed twin-towered Lighthouse (one
tower blind) where the quality of hopscotch, on a slab of slate
near the chief engineer's lodgings, must have been unexampled
in the West. So back at length, above Polpeor and what used to be
the lifeboat station, to Pistol, the mountain-wall of Rocky Lane,

our fuchsia-drive, and the conspicuous pink house with its wide and welcoming back-door.

That evening, no doubt, the postman would arrive at the same door, an aged, bearded, and sententious man who had been in foreign parts—I believe Australia—and was almost excessively literate. He had a stately voice with a roll in it; lit by a bulls-eye lantern, he walked on dark nights in a one-man progress. As a rule he would offer, in his organ-diapason, a brief commentary on the current letters. 'Good Evening, All,' he would say with unction, and in capitals: 'A Raw Night. Here is a Letter for you from Plymouth. Another, I surmise, from the North, and—ah! yes!— a Picture Postcard from the Captain. H'm! . . . A lively American scene. And here too is a Parcel, a Long, Flat Parcel . . .' So he rumbled on (while I hid beneath the table) until Good Night was proclaimed, trumpets probably sounded in the distance, and the lantern would wink and weave up the drive.

He was a favourite character. Others were my uncle by marriage, who insisted on reciting Milton to me while he was weeding the lawn; a cobbler, wedged into his tiny room like a walnut in its shell; a muscular, swarthy man who had a Spanish name, pronounced as spelt, and the trick of carrying on any conversation at a range of two hundred yards; and a First Witch (quite harmless) from mid-village. She spent her time combing the beaches for driftwood or any of the flotsam—it varied between corks, oranges, and the rubber teats of fountain-pen fillers—that the sea might toss up between Housel and Caerthillian.

The sea was our first thought. The calendar moved from wreck to wreck—'Hansy year' or 'Just before the Cromdale'. For me, one spring was when the barque Queen Margaret, like a great white bird, came too close inshore on an oiled-silk morning, and from the hedge-path to Polpeor we saw her masts slant, totter, and fall.

In stormy, or 'coarse', January weather, each cliff and beach had its individual note: a dynamiting, pile-driving boom against the full face of Old Lizard Head; the boiling hiss, as of a sea-serpent, among the rocks and pools of Pistol Cove; a growl, swooping yet protracted, as wave upon wave drove, white to the lips, across the shelving sand of Pentreath. There were places, too—the crest of Rocky Lane was one—where the sea appeared to be running downhill to meet you. You were level then with

the horizon. By the time you reached Pistol Meadow, the stile
with its serpentine slabs and the hummocked grass, water should
have been pouring over you in a cascade. But it never did.

Father, bred in sail and without a quiver of nerves at any height,
would walk across to Kynance and the Rill, keeping—I thought—
to the extreme verge of the cliff. I was not made for heights,
though with other village boys I would go scrambling now and
again, knowing what it meant to be spread against a steep rock-
face, sustained by the pressure of a boot-nail, and looking down
to see the waves foam and flake, arch and tighten. It happened
seldom. The Lizard was a world of daunting precipices, of cornices
on which only a mountain goat would perch. I continue to shiver
at the plight of the botanist-topographer, C. A. Johns, who
nearly a century-and-a-half ago tried to scale the cliffs by Gue
Graze and found himself, after eighty feet or so, dangling by his
finger-tips:

> Feeling that I could hold no longer by my fingers, I made a
> violent effort and planted my knee, I know not how, just
> below my hands; still, I was not safe. I was now balanced on
> my hands and one knee on the edge of the cliff—one leg was
> still hanging over idle—and my book, which I had not the
> means of getting rid of, had slipped round in front and inserted
> itself between my body and the rock.

He was only half-way up, but he did get to the top—rather an
anti-climax that reminded me of the serial convention, 'One
bound and our hero was free'.

So much returns: from shore and cliff and sea, village and lane:
the hum of the serpentine-turners' wheels in an early winter dusk;
the faded brocade of salt-stiff turf; the broad 'double hedges' on
which we could go towards Kynance or Cadgwith and Ruan
Minor (at The Lizard men would be as trees walking); a parliament
of gulls on our lawn; the sound of Landewednack rookery at
evening; the Cornish tale of *Moyar Diu* read on Pentreath; the
Col'para (or Colperro) custom when each Shrove Tuesday we
went from door to door, gathering a harvest of biscuits, buns and
sweets; the escalading, darting rush of coastline from Old Lizard
to the Rill; the foghorn's metallic moo; sloe-gathering in a lane

behind the church; the rush one summer morning—and the only time in my experience—to put up a Union flag in the well between our central attic windows as Father's ship steamed past The Lizard and he returned our signal. I spent the rest of that morning on the Head, hoping he might pass again . . .

HENRY WILLIAMSON

Home Ground

Henry Williamson's son, Richard Williamson, writes:

The following extract is from *The Pathway*, the fourth and final volume of the tetralogy, *The Flax of Dream*. It was first published in 1929, after *Tarka the Otter* and before *Salar the Salmon*. It is a passionate recognition of the North Devon seaboard from Hartland Point to Lynmouth, the country which gave him nearly all of his finest books, and which nursed him back to health after four years in the trenches of the First World War.

Henry loved Exeter, and was a frequent visitor to the Cathedral where he often wrote, inspired by his surroundings and music from the organ or a concert. It was to Exeter University that he presented the 'Devon' manuscripts, including that of *Tarka the Otter*, long before his death.

Already, as he was crossing the Great Field, the stars seemed more remote, their beams shortened and steady; the avalanche of darkness was moving away from the world. He felt as immense as the firmament, and filled with a vast impersonal joy. Eosphoros, the Morning Star, bright witness to the visions of men, would soon be bringing the dawn over Dunkery Beacon, and he must see it from the hills. He walked swiftly, with long strides, crossing the eastern corner of the Great Field to the road that led to the modern houses of Santon, and, rising thence above the sea-sloping fields of Down End, turned through the rock inland to Cryde, past the sands of the bay.

He followed the road for a quarter of a mile, and vaulting over a gate, crossed a field of stubble, while the first shrill music of a lark dropped in the dimming night. Now Shelley was in the wind and the grasses of the hedge with him, and Jefferies free of the world's negation, and Blake, and Thompson, and Jesus of Nazareth, and his shoulders were wide as the hills, and his spirit strong as the sea, for they said as they moved beside him, We are with you evermore, for you are of us! And he strode faster, with open mouth to draw down the skin of his face, until the hindering tears had run from his eyes.

The songs of larks began to fall as rain in the lessening darkness, as he pushed through a thorn hedge and dropped into a sunken lane, and climbed the steep bank into a higher field. Brambles of wild rose hooked his coat and scratched his hands and ankles, but he hardly felt them. A pair of horses snorted somewhere near him, and their grey shapes fled away with thudding hooves. Soon he had crossed the field, and was pulling himself up another steep bank by the branches of an ash-tree, which had been half-cut and laid along the hedge.

He ran along the headland of a field near Lobb Farm, leaping over the withering plants of musk thistles and cracking the stems of hemlock fallen with old summer weight out of the bank. Through another hedge he broke, heedless of the stabs of the little gnarled wind-savage blackthorns that hardly yielded before him. He must reach the highest point of the down before sunrise!

By a broken gate that flapped to his weight on a rotting post of a planted ship's rib, he stopped, and looked up. The inert heaviness was gone from the night; the darkness was a-stir, lightless light was moving everywhere over the fields, passing through and charging with its mystic power every branch and stone and leaf of clover. The sky seemed to deepen and to glow with a translucent blue that was an illimitable and perpetual joyousness and safety for all life. He breathed deeply, and with the outward breath released himself into the light, wan and pure, of all-knowing. He felt himself of the everlasting life and light of the world.

A tree stood beside him, a pollard oak whose flank had been

opened and smoothed with an axe, to make swinging way for the gate. An iron staple was driven deep into its old wound, which had long since healed. He put his arms round the trunk, and pressing his cheek on the hard ridges of the bark, felt the presence of a gentle spirit within the sappy bole. Dear tree, he thought with a sudden and tranquil sadness, we shall never see each other again; and he opened the gate and went up a lane no wider than a cart, whose rocky surface was deeply grooved by the iron of labouring feet of the centuries. At a bend in the lane he looked back, and sent a last thought to his unknown friend.

The rusty-edged leaves of the thorn hedge above the sunken lane began to rustle and the wind to touch his face. He reached the top of the lane, which ended at another gate, and clambering over, was in a stony field on whose poor grass sheep were feeding.

The dawn! The higher ground of the next field grew darker, and the sky just above the hill-line glowed with pale yellow, making the distant trees of Windwhistle Spinney black and distinct. Above the primrose bar light from under the earth's rim flowed to the starry zenith, with a startling loveliness and water-likeness. The sun was remote; yonder was the light of the world, while he, an aspiring mortal, stood in the dusky field and looked at the Morning Star, raptured to the lips. Mother of Keats's spirit, of the world-free Shelley, the broken-winged bird that was Thompson, of Jefferies who was a leaf and a feather and the sea— the Morning Star walked in her whiteness up the sky, the Mother of Life who had led the mighty beams to run with laughter over the heavens, and now was soon to wither, and her spirit to flow back into the sunlight.

The wind blew cold on the hill, and when he turned and faced the west the sky before him was dark and terrible, for clouds were travelling over the Atlantic. The western darkness seemed without life, until out of the darkness invisible things cried harshly, as though insanely, seeming to mock the Morning Star which had shrunk and lost its brimming lustre. They were gulls from the headland, coming inland to seek food in the fields. Then down the hedge a whiteness floated silently, and fell fluttering on a lark that had just dropped from its song to the morning. The owl flew away with the lark in its talons, and glided to earth beyond the farther hedge.

A change came over him immediately.

'That is reality; not my way,' he thought, and the feeling of greatness and joy went from him.

He asked himself why he was walking in the field; and what would he see when he reached the end of the down he had been making for so quickly. Only the heathery slope down to the cliffs and the sea. He had walked there many times before, and knew what was to be seen in clear air—the Welsh coast to the north, Lundy and the Atlantic to the west, and Dartmoor to the south; he knew every flower, bird, fern, grass, rock, animal, bush; and the vain and empty sky over all.

He looked over the Burrows, which lay spectral and flat below the hill. He thought of them sleeping there so tranquilly—the normal human life. He saw Mary's head on the pillow, and as he brooded on the sweet vision a piercing anguish arose in his heart. The power which had gone forth into the sky was now directed to Mary, and made her smile, and open her eyes, and put forth her warm arms and draw down his head and cherish it on her breast. He sat down on a cold stone, and wept, having no hope.

Afterwards he reproached himself for being weak, and walked on, waiting for the sun. The air was now faintly roaring again; a grey mist of spray becoming visible over the Pebble Ridge across the estuary, and a white thin smear of waves in the wide sea-mouth of the rivers. The lights of earth and heaven were equal.

He came to the end of the down, to ground unbroken by plough or mattock, and rough with fern and bramble; and the sun came up, spreading its first pale gold on the rimed grasses, and laying long shadows behind the furze. In a brighter and more open air he began to hope again as he looked at the scene of those happy summer days now ended. The land dropped away below his feet—the estuary and the Branton pill were filled with shining sea; the Great Field, shorn of its Joseph's-coat of summer corn-colours, lay sere and autumnal; the heave and waste of the sand-hills, with their yellowing grasses; the level sands bending round Aery Point, the sea wrinkled like an elephant's hide, but shining; the long blue length of land that stretched into that sea, anciently called Hercules Promontory.

A low sweep of the hand and forearm covered the entire visible land and sea. With such a gesture of the mind he would sweep

away all the world of men, and replace it with his own vision—
the incommunicable vision he used to call the White Bird. He
shielded his eyes, and looked at the ring of trees enclosing a
minute smudge which was the thatched roof of Wildernesse,
three miles away as the falcon glided. Mary would be dressed
now: perhaps leaving her work, and wandering forth to look for
mushrooms. Perhaps she was at that moment looking at the hills,
wondering if he were there, and thinking of him; but he could
not go to seek her, for so he had promised her mother.

He remained on the hills at noon, sometimes lying on his back
and dozing, or gazing at the sky through the shutter of his hands.
There was no wind; the sea and the sky shared a deep blue; the
earth was warm and calm with the mellow autumn sun. He
thought of the cider that he and Uncle Sufford were to make;
now was the cider-sun, and dry apple-picking time: and Mary,
in her old school gym-suit, might be gathering apples—but he was
not with her in the lichen-shaggy boughs, while the appledranes
ate the sweetest apples hollow. Appledrane, appledrone, beautiful
childlike descriptive word of simple men—the wasps droning
round the hollow apples, in the warm, mellow, cider-sparkling
autumn air. Bideford Bay was horizoned with mist; a collier was
passing through a burnished shield on the sea. England, so beautiful,
so inexpressibly beautiful!

Gossamer gleamed in the fields of stubble, in shining paths under
the sun; and through the air came the sad-sweet song of a wood-
lark, singing unseen from clod or ditched stone wall. The bird was
little and drab, it mattered not where or what it was; there was
genius in the song, a hymn to the life-giving sun, to the light.

In the afternoon he walked down Sky Lane leading over the
hill to the Burrows, by which farmers of olden time had brought
their corn from the inland valleys to be winnowed by the wind
in the sand-hills. When last he had walked there, on Easter Sunday
morning, the bines of the bryony had been pushing with spring
fervour their long green slow-worm-like heads through blackthorn
and bramble; the way was joyful with the wings of linnets and
finches. Now the fruit of the bryony trailed in strings of withering
red and yellow berries and all song was silent along that ancient
sunken sled-track. Near the Santon road he stopped, and looked

back in farewell. Faintly over the sloping fields came the slow-falling song of the solitary wood-lark. Lovely little immortal, he could hear God in its throat-strings.

He walked to the sea, where the lines of waves rearing to fall were burnished by the southern sun, and the foam carried the shattered sparkle up the wet sands. As he was walking over the crest of a sand-hill, after a swim in the sea, he saw figures on Ferny Hill; and sinking down on a mat of wild thyme, beside mullein stalks grey and dry, he watched what appeared to be a hawking party. Mr Chychester was there, with Mrs Ogilvie, Howard, Pamela, Ronnie, and other people, including what was apparently a keeper standing apart from them. Two black specks were aloft, peregrine falcons at their pitches, waiting on for partridges to be put up by the spaniels working through the bracken. A magpie flew up. He saw the black and white flicker of wings before it sloped to earth again, when one of the black specks fell and swooped up, to hang still at its pitch.

His heart thudded as he decided to go straight to them, and ask Mary to come with him, as a falcon, espying its mate, cut the air unswerving and heedless of any bird that flew! While he hesitated a dog flushed the magpie again: the other falcon stooped: he heard the thud of the smitten bird, and saw the burst of feathers hang in the still air. Poor magpie! And thinking of Mrs Ogilvie, he went away unseen.

He crossed the marsh, and walked by the sea-wall. The long summer grasses were yellow and drooping, the thistle cardoons broken and flossy with seed, the sorrel spires dry and brown. In the clayey spaces between the stones leading down to the saltings the leaves of the sea-beet were reddening to drink more of the sun. The tide was creeping over the saltings, shaking the wildered blooms of the Michaelmas daisies, and pouring into the channels and locked pools in the sodden turf.

By the harp-bend of the wall, where the pill merged into the wide estuary, he stood and watched a ketch riding up on the flood. Its sails hung slack; the metallic thuds of its engine, fouling the air, were echoed flatly from over the marsh and the estuary. It turned into the pill, stuck on a sand-bank, and began to swing round with the flood. He listened to the good-humoured chaff of the three men on deck, accompanied by the usual meaningless bloodies, while they waited for the tide to 'rise' them. A mongrel dog sat contentedly on a hatch and watched the water.

With regret he saw the ship float free, and move away, while the long-tailed mongrel dog ran up and down the deck barking with joy as it met again the familiar smells lying stagnant between the walls of the pill. He remembered his own dog, which had slipped away when he had left the cottage, tormented by its own vision and desire; and he thought to return to the village and look for Billjohn, but an unaccountable reluctance overcame the thought. He must see the sun sink away into the sea, as he had watched it rising. O sun, mighty life-giver, he thought, the tears started by his inner strength: let man try to crucify thee, and he will learn who is God! And even as thou must tread the sky, so must I tread the way, narrow and dark, to the shining truth that is the light of Khristos.

The excitation of this thought, and its consequent calm, did not endure beyond a lapse of a few minutes; and his longing for the love and tenderness of Mary increased as the sun went down. With strange sense of foreboding he saw the blinding haze dissolving the Burrows shrink into the line of the sand-hills. He stood on the wall until the sun had set, and only the afterglow remained; and then he went into Luke's hut, as though to find refuge from an indefinable dread.

AGATHA CHRISTIE

The Regatta Mystery

This story, set in Dartmouth, South Devon, and one of a collection under the general title of *The Regatta Mystery*, was published in 1939. In that year the late Dame Agatha—who has been called affectionately 'The First Lady of Crime'—and her husband, (Sir) Max Mallowan, bought Greenway House by the upper reaches of the Dart.

Mr Isaac Pointz removed a cigar from his lips and said approvingly:
    'Pretty little place.'
    Having thus set the seal of his approval upon Dartmouth harbour, he replaced the cigar and looked about him with the air of a man pleased with himself, his appearance, his surroundings and life generally.
    As regards the first of these, Mr Isaac Pointz was a man of fifty-eight, in good health and condition with perhaps a slight tendency to liver. He was not exactly stout, but comfortable-looking, and a yachting costume, which he wore at the moment, is not the most kindly of attires for a middle-aged man with a tendency to embonpoint. Mr Pointz was very well turned out—correct to every crease and button—his dark and slightly Oriental face beaming out under the peak of his yachting cap. As regards his surroundings, these may have been taken to mean his companions—his partner Mr Leo Stein, Sir George and Lady Marro-

way, an American business acquaintance Mr Samuel Leathern and his schoolgirl daughter Eve, Mrs Rustington and Evan Llewellyn.

The party had just come ashore from Mr Pointz's yacht—the *Merrimaid*. In the morning they had watched the yacht racing and they had now come ashore to join for a while in the fun of the fair—Coconut shies, Fat Ladies, the Human Spider and the Merry-go-round. It is hardly to be doubted that these delights were relished most by Eve Leathern. When Mr Pointz finally suggested that it was time to adjourn to the Royal George for dinner, hers was the only dissentient voice.

'Oh, Mr Pointz—I did so want to have my fortune told by the Real Gypsy in the Caravan.'

Mr Pointz had doubts of the essential Realness of the Gypsy in question but he gave indulgent assent.

'Eve's just crazy about the fair,' said her father apologetically. 'But don't you pay any attention if you want to be getting along.'

'Plenty of time,' said Mr Pointz benignantly. 'Let the little lady enjoy herself. I'll take you on at darts, Leo.'

'Twenty-five and over wins a prize,' chanted the man in charge of the darts in a high nasal voice.

'Bet you a fiver my total score beats yours,' said Pointz.

'Done,' said Stein with alacrity.

The two men were soon whole-heartedly engaged in their battle.

Lady Marroway murmured to Evan Llewellyn:

'Eve is not the only child in the party.'

Llewellyn smiled assent but somewhat absently.

He had been absent-minded all that day. Once or twice his answers had been wide of the point.

Pamela Marroway drew away from him and said to her husband:

'That young man has something on his mind.'

Sir George murmured:

'Or someone?'

And his glance swept quickly over Janet Rustington.

Lady Marroway frowned a little. She was a tall woman exquisitely groomed. The scarlet of her fingernails was matched by the dark red coral studs in her ears. Her eyes were dark and watchful. Sir George affected a careless 'hearty English gentleman' manner—but his bright blue eyes held the same watchful look as his wife's.

Isaac Pointz and Leo Stein were Hatton Garden diamond merchants. Sir George and Lady Marroway came from a different world—the world of Antibes and Juan les Pins—of golf at St-Jean-de-Luz—of bathing from the rocks at Madeira in the winter.

In outward seeming they were as the lilies that toiled not, neither did they spin. But perhaps this was not quite true. There are divers ways of toiling and also of spinning.

'Here's the kid back again,' said Evan Llewellyn to Mrs Rustington.

He was a dark young man—there was a faintly hungry wolfish look about him which some women found attractive.

It was difficult to say whether Mrs Rustington found him so. She did not wear her heart on her sleeve. She had married young —and the marriage had ended in disaster in less than a year. Since that time it was difficult to know what Janet Rustington thought of anyone or anything—her manner was always the same —charming but completely aloof.

Eve Leathern came dancing up to them, her lank fair hair bobbing excitedly. She was fifteen—an awkward child—but full of vitality.

'I'm going to be married by the time I'm seventeen,' she exclaimed breathlessly. 'To a very rich man and we're going to have six children and Tuesdays and Thursdays are my lucky days and I ought always to wear green or blue and an emerald is my lucky stone and—'

'Why, pet, I think we ought to be getting along,' said her father.

Mr Leathern was a tall, fair, dyspeptic-looking man with a somewhat mournful expression.

Mr Pointz and Mr Stein were turning away from the darts. Mr Pointz was chuckling and Mr Stein was looking somewhat rueful.

'It's all a matter of luck,' he was saying.

Mr Pointz slapped his pocket cheerfully.

'Took a fiver off you all right. Skill, my boy, skill. My old Dad was a first-class dart player. Well, folks, let's be getting along. Had your fortune told, Eve? Did they tell you to beware of a dark man?'

'A dark woman,' corrected Eve. 'She's got a cast in her eye and she'll be real mean to me if I give her a chance. And I'm to be married by the time I'm seventeen . . .'

She ran on happily as the party steered its way to the Royal George.

Dinner had been ordered beforehand by the forethought of Mr Pointz and a bowing waiter led them upstairs and into a private room on the first floor. Here a round table was ready laid. The big bulging bow-window opened on the harbour square and was open. The noise of the fair came up to them, and the raucous squeal of three roundabouts each blaring a different tune.

'Best shut that if we're to hear ourselves speak,' observed Mr Pointz drily, and suited the action to the word.

They took their seats round the table and Mr Pointz beamed affectionately at his guests. He felt he was doing them well and he liked to do people well. His eye rested on one after another. Lady Marroway—fine woman—not quite the goods, of course, he knew that—he was perfectly well aware that what he had called all his life the *crème de la crème* would have very little to do with the Marroways—but then the *crème de la crème* were supremely unaware of his own existence. Anyway, Lady Marroway was a damned smart-looking woman—and he didn't mind if she *did* rook him at Bridge. Didn't enjoy it quite so much from Sir George. Fishy eye the fellow had. Brazenly on the make. But he wouldn't make too much out of Isaac Pointz. He'd see to that all right.

Old Leathern wasn't a bad fellow—long-winded, of course, like most Americans—fond of telling endless long stories. And he had that disconcerting habit of requiring precise information. What was the population of Dartmouth? In what year had the Naval College been built? And so on. Expected his host to be a kind of walking Baedeker. Eve was a nice cheery kid—he enjoyed chaffing her. Voice rather like a corncrake, but she had all her wits about her. A bright kid.

Young Llewellyn—he seemed a bit quiet. Looked as though he had something on his mind. Hard up, probably. These writing fellows usually were. Looked as though he might be keen on Janet Rustington. A nice woman—attractive and clever, too. But she didn't ram her writing down your throat. Highbrow sort of stuff she wrote but you'd never think it to hear her talk. And old Leo! *He* wasn't getting younger or thinner. And blissfully unaware that his partner was at that moment thinking precisely the same thing about him, Mr Pointz corrected Mr Leathern as to pilchards being connected with Devon and not Cornwall, and prepared to enjoy his dinner.

'Mr Pointz,' said Eve when plates of hot mackerel had been set before them and the waiters had left the room.

'Yes, young lady.'

'Have you got that big diamond with you right now? The one you showed us last night and said you always took about with you?'

Mr Pointz chuckled.

'That's right. My mascot, I call it. Yes, I've got it with me all right.'

'I think that's awfully dangerous. Somebody might get it away from you in the crowd at the fair.'

'Not they,' said Mr Pointz. 'I'll take good care of that.'

'But they *might*,' insisted Eve. 'You've got gangsters in England as well as we have, haven't you?'

'They won't get the Morning Star,' said Mr Pointz. 'To begin with it's in a special inner pocket. And anyway—old Pointz knows what he's about. Nobody's going to steal the Morning Star.'

Eve laughed.

'Ugh-huh—bet I could steal it!'

'I bet you couldn't,' Mr Pointz twinkled back at her.

'Well, I bet I could. I was thinking about it last night in bed— after you'd handed it round the table for us all to look at. I thought of a real cute way to steal it.'

'And what's that?'

Eve put her head on one side, her fair hair wagged excitedly. 'I'm not telling you—now. What do you bet I couldn't?'

Memories of Mr Pointz's youth rose in his mind.

'Half a dozen pairs of gloves,' he said.

'Gloves,' cried Eve disgustedly. 'Who wears gloves?'

'Well—do you wear nylon stockings?'

'Do I not? My best pair ran this morning.'

'Very well, then. Half a dozen pairs of the finest nylon stockings—'

'Oo-er,' said Eve blissfully. 'And what about you?'

'Well, I need a new tobacco pouch.'

'Right. That's a deal. Not that you'll get your tobacco pouch. Now I'll tell you what you've got to do. You must hand it round like you did last night—'

She broke off as two waiters entered to remove the plates. When they were starting on the next course of chicken, Mr Pointz said:

'Remember this, young woman, if this is to represent a real theft, I should send for the police and you'd be searched.'

'That's quite OK by me. You needn't be quite so lifelike as to bring the police into it. But Lady Marroway or Mrs Rustington can do all the searching you like.'

'Well, that's that then,' said Mr Pointz. 'What are you setting up to be? A first-class jewel thief?'

'I might take to it as a career—if it really paid.'

'If you got away with the Morning Star it would pay you. Even after recutting that stone would be worth over thirty thousand pounds.'

'My!' said Eve, impressed. 'What's that in dollars?'

Lady Marroway uttered an exclamation.

'And you carry such a stone about with you?' she said reproachfully. 'Thirty thousand pounds.' Her darkened eyelashes quivered.

Mrs Rustington said softly: 'It's a lot of money . . . And then there's the fascination of the stone itself . . . It's beautiful.'

'Just a piece of carbon,' said Evan Llewellyn.

'I've always understood it's the "fence" that's the difficulty in jewel robberies,' said Sir George. 'He takes the lion's share—eh, what?'

'Come on,' said Eve excitedly. 'Let's start. Take the diamond out and say what you said last night.'

Mr Leathern said in his deep melancholy voice, 'I do apologise for my offspring. She gets kinder worked up—'

'That'll do, Pops,' said Eve. 'Now then, Mr Pointz—'

Smiling, Mr Pointz fumbled in an inner pocket. He drew something out. It lay on the palm of his hand, blinking in the light.

A diamond . . .

Rather stiffly, Mr Pointz repeated as far as he could remember his speech of the previous evening on the *Merrimaid*.

'Perhaps you ladies and gentlemen would like to have a look at this? It's an unusually beautiful stone. I call it the Morning Star and it's by way of being my mascot—goes about with me anywhere. Like to see it?'

He handed it to Lady Marroway, who took it, exclaimed at its beauty and passed it to Mr Leathern who said, 'Pretty good— yes, pretty good,' in a somewhat artificial manner and in his turn passed it to Llewellyn.

The waiters coming in at that moment, there was a slight hitch in the proceedings. When they had gone again, Evan said, 'Very fine stone' and passed it to Leo Stein who did not trouble to make any comment but handed it quickly on to Eve.

'How perfectly lovely,' cried Eve in a high affected voice.

'Oh!' She gave a cry of consternation as it slipped from her hand. 'I've dropped it.'

She pushed back her chair and got down to grope under the table. Sir George at her right, bent also. A glass got swept off the table in the confusion. Stein, Llewellyn and Mrs Rustington all helped in the search. Finally Lady Marroway joined in.

Only Mr Pointz took no part in the proceedings. He remained in his seat sipping his wine and smiling sardonically.

'Oh, dear,' said Eve, still in her artificial manner. 'How dreadful! Where *can* it have rolled to? I can't find it anywhere.'

One by one the assistant searchers rose to their feet.

'It's disappeared all right, Pointz,' said Sir George smiling.

'Very nicely done,' said Mr Pointz, nodding approval. 'You'd make a very good actress, Eve. Now the question is, have you hidden it somewhere or have you got it on you?'

'Search me,' said Eve dramatically.

Mr Pointz's eye sought out a large screen in the corner of the room.

He nodded towards it and then looked at Lady Marroway and Mrs Rustington.

'If you ladies will be so good—'

'Why, certainly,' said Lady Marroway, smiling.

The two women rose.

Lady Marroway said,

'Don't be afraid, Mr Pointz, we'll vet her properly.'

The three went behind the screen.

The room was hot. Evan Llewellyn flung open the window. A news vendor was passing. Evan threw down a coin and the man threw up a paper.

Llewellyn unfolded it.

'Hungarian situation's none too good,' he said.

'That the local rag?' asked Sir George. 'There's a horse I'm interested in ought to have run at Haldon today—Natty Boy.'

'Leo,' said Mr Pointz. 'Lock the door. We don't want those damned waiters popping in and out till this business is over.'

'Natty Boy won three to one,' said Evan.

'Rotten odds,' said Sir George.

'Mostly Regatta news,' said Evan, glancing over the sheet.

The three young women came out from the screen.

'Not a sign of it,' said Janet Rustington.

'You can take it from me she hasn't got it on her,' said Lady Marroway.

Mr Pointz thought he would be quite ready to take it from her. There was a grim tone in her voice and he felt no doubt that the search had been thorough.

'Say, Eve, you haven't swallowed it?' asked Mr Leathern anxiously. 'Because maybe that wouldn't be too good for you.'

'I'd have seen her do that,' said Leo Stein quietly. 'I was watching her. She didn't put anything in her mouth.'

'I couldn't swallow a great thing all points like that,' said Eve. She put her hands on her hips and looked at Mr Pointz. 'What about it, big boy?' she asked.

'You stand over there where you are and don't move,' said that gentleman.

Among them, the men stripped the table and turned it upside down. Mr Pointz examined every inch of it. Then he transferred his attention to the chair on which Eve had been sitting and those on either side of her.

The thoroughness of the search left nothing to be desired. The other four men joined in and the women also. Eve Leathern stood by the wall near the screen and laughed with intense enjoyment.

Five minutes later Mr Pointz rose with a slight groan from his knees and dusted his trousers sadly. His pristine freshness was somewhat impaired.

'Eve,' he said. 'I take off my hat to you. You're the finest thing in jewel thieves I've ever come across. What you've done with that stone beats me. As far as I can see it must be in the room as it isn't on you. I give you best.'

'Are the stockings mine?' demanded Eve.

'They're yours, young lady.'

'Eve, my child, where *can* you have hidden it?' demanded Mrs Rustington curiously.

Eve pranced forward.

'I'll show you. You'll all be just mad with yourselves.'

She went across to the side table where the things from the dinner table had been roughly stacked. She picked up her little black evening bag—

'Right under your eyes. Right . . .'

Her voice, gay and triumphant, trailed off suddenly.

'Oh,' she said. '*Oh* . . .'

'What's the matter, honey?' said her father.

Eve whispered: 'It's gone . . . it's *gone* . . .'

'What's all this?' asked Pointz, coming forward.

Eve turned to him impetuously.

'It was like this. This pochette of mine has a big paste stone in the middle of the clasp. It fell out last night and just when you were showing that diamond round I noticed that it was much the same size. And so I thought in the night what a good idea for a robbery it would be to wedge your diamond into the gap with a bit of plasticine. I felt sure nobody would ever spot it. That's what I did tonight. First I dropped it—then went down after it with the bag in my hand, stuck it into the gap with a bit of plasticine which I had handy, put my bag on the table and went on pretending to look for the diamond. I thought it would be like the Purloined Letter—you know—lying there in full view under all your noses—and just looking like a common bit of rhinestone. And it was a good plan—none of you *did* notice.'

'I wonder,' said Mr Stein.

'What did you say?'

Mr Pointz took the bag, looked at the empty hole with a fragment of plasticine still adhering to it and said slowly: 'It may have fallen out. We'd better look again.'

The search was repeated, but this time it was a curiously silent business. An atmosphere of tension pervaded the room.

Finally everyone in turn gave it up. They stood looking at each other.

'It's not in this room,' said Stein.

'And nobody's left the room,' said Sir George significantly.

There was a moment's pause. Eve burst into tears.

Her father patted her on the shoulder.

'There, there,' he said awkwardly.

Sir George turned to Leo Stein.

'Mr Stein,' he said. 'Just now you murmured something under your breath. When I asked you to repeat it, you said it was nothing. But as a matter of fact I heard what you said. Miss Eve had just said that none of us noticed the place where she had put the diamond. The words you murmured were: "I wonder." What we have to face is the probability that one person *did* notice—that that person is in this room now. I suggest that the only fair and honourable thing is for every one present to submit to a search. The diamond cannot have left the room.'

When Sir George played the part of the old English gentleman, none could play it better. His voice rang with sincerity and indignation.

'Bit unpleasant, all this,' said Mr Pointz unhappily.

'It's all my fault,' sobbed Eve. 'I didn't mean—'

'Buck up, kiddo,' said Mr Stein kindly. 'Nobody's blaming you.'

Mr Leathern said in his slow pedantic manner:

'Why, certainly, I think that Sir George's suggestion will meet with the fullest approval from all of us. It does from me.'

'I agree,' said Evan Llewellyn.

Mrs Rustington looked at Lady Marroway who nodded a brief assent. The two of them went back behind the screen and the sobbing Eve accompanied them.

A waiter knocked on the door and was told to go away.

Five minutes later eight people looked at each other incredulously.

The Morning Star had vanished into space . . .

Mr Parker Pyne looked thoughtfully at the dark agitated face of the young man opposite him.

'Of course,' he said. 'You're Welsh, Mr Llewellyn.'

'What's that got to do with it?'

Mr Parker Pyne waved a large, well-cared-for hand.

'Nothing at all, I admit. I am interested in the classification of emotional reactions as exemplified by certain racial types. That is all. Let us return to the consideration of your particular problem.'

'I don't really know why I came to you,' said Evan Llewellyn. His hands twitched nervously, and his dark face had a haggard look. He did not look at Mr Parker Pyne and that gentleman's scrutiny seemed to make him uncomfortable. 'I don't know why I came to you,' he repeated. 'But where the Hell *can* I go? And what the Hell can I *do*? It's the powerlessness of not being able to do anything at all that gets me . . . I saw your advertisement and I remembered that a chap had once spoken of you and said that you got results . . . And—well—I came! I suppose I was a fool. It's the sort of position nobody can do anything about.'

'Not at all,' said Mr Parker Pyne. 'I am the proper person to come to. I am a specialist in unhappiness. This business has obviously caused you a good deal of pain. You are sure the facts are exactly as you have told me?'

'I don't think I've left out anything. Pointz brought out the diamond and passed it around—that wretched American child stuck it on her ridiculous bag and when we came to look at the bag, the diamond was gone. It wasn't on anyone—old Pointz himself even was searched—he suggested it himself—and I'll swear it was nowhere in that room! *And nobody left the room—*'

No waiters, for instance?' suggested Mr Parker Pyne.

Llewellyn shook his head.

'They went out before the girl began messing about with the diamond, and afterwards Pointz locked the door so as to keep them out. No, it lies between one of us.'

'It would certainly seem so,' said Mr Parker Pyne thoughtfully.

'That damned evening paper,' said Evan Llewellyn bitterly. 'I saw it come into their minds—that that was the only way—'

'Just tell me again exactly what occurred.'

'It was perfectly simple. I threw open the window, whistled to the man, threw down a copper and he tossed me up the paper. And there it is, you see—the only possible way the diamond could have left the room—thrown by me to an accomplice waiting in the street below.'

'Not the *only* possible way,' said Mr Parker Pyne.

'What other way can you suggest?'

'If you didn't throw it out, there *must* have been some other way.'

'Oh, I see. I hoped you meant something more definite than that. Well, I can only say that I *didn't* throw it out. I can't expect you to believe me—or anyone else.'

'Oh, yes, I believe you,' said Mr Parker Pyne.

'You do? Why?'

'Not a criminal type,' said Mr Parker Pyne. 'Not, that is, the particular criminal type that steals jewellery. There are crimes, of course, that you might commit—but we won't enter into that subject At any rate I do not see you as the purloiner of the Morning Star.'

'Everyone else does though,' said Llewellyn bitterly.

'I see,' said Mr Parker Pyne.

'They looked at me in a queer sort of way at the time. Marroway picked up the paper and just glanced over at the window. He didn't say anything. But Pointz cottoned on to it quick enough! I could see what they thought. There hasn't been any open accusation, that's the devil of it.'

Mr Parker Pyne nodded sympathetically.

'It is worse than that,' he said.

'Yes. It's just suspicion. I've had a fellow round asking questions —routine inquiries, he called it. One of the new dress-shirted lot of police, I suppose. Very tactful—nothing at all hinted. Just interested in the fact that I'd been hard up and was suddenly cutting a bit of a splash.'

'And were you?'

'Yes—some luck with a horse or two. Unluckily my bets were made on the course—there's nothing to show that that's how the money came in. They can't disprove it, of course—but that's just the sort of easy lie a fellow would invent if he didn't want to show where the money came from.'

'I agree. Still they will have to have a good deal more than that to go upon.'

'Oh! I'm not afraid of actually being arrested and charged with the theft. In a way that would be easier—one would know where one was. It's the ghastly fact that all those people believe I took it.'

'One person in particular?'

'What do you mean?'

'A suggestion—nothing more—' Again Mr Parker Pyne waved his comfortable-looking hand. 'There *was* one person in particular, wasn't there? Shall we say Mrs Rustington?'

Llewellyn's dark face flushed.

'Why pitch on her?'

'Oh, my dear sir—there is obviously someone whose opinion matters to you greatly—probably a lady. What ladies were there? An American flapper? Lady Marroway? But you would probably rise not fall in Lady Marroway's estimation if you had brought off such a coup. I know something of the lady. Clearly then, Mrs Rustington.'

Llewellyn said with something of an effort,

'She—she's had rather an unfortunate experience. Her husband was a down and out rotter. It's made her unwilling to trust anyone. She—if she thinks—'

He found it difficult to go on.

'Quite so,' said Mr Parker Pyne. 'I see the matter is important. It must be cleared up.'

Evan gave a short laugh.

'That's easy to say.'

'And quite easy to do,' said Mr Parker Pyne.

'You think so?'

'Oh, yes—the problem is so clear-cut. So many possibilities are ruled out. The answer must really be extremely simple. Indeed already I have a kind of glimmering—'

Llewellyn stared at him incredulously.

Mr Parker Pyne drew a pad of paper towards him and picked up a pen.

'Perhaps you would give me a brief description of the party.'

'Haven't I already done so?'

'Their personal appearance—colour of hair and so on.'

'But, Mr Parker Pyne, what can that have to do with it?'

'A good deal, young man, a good deal. Classification and so on.'

Somewhat unbelievingly, Evan described the personal appearance of the members of the yachting party.

Mr Parker Pyne made a note or two, pushed away the pad and said:

'Excellent. By the way, did you say a wine-glass was broken?'

Evan stared again.

'Yes, it was knocked off the table and then it got stepped on.'

'Nasty thing, splinters of glass,' said Mr Parker Pyne. 'Whose wine-glass was it?'

'I think it was the child's—Eve.'

'Ah!—and who sat next to her on that side?'

'Sir George Marroway.'

'You didn't see which of them knocked it off the table?'

'Afraid I didn't. Does it matter?'

'Not really. No. That was a superfluous question. Well'—he stood up—'good morning, Mr Llewellyn. Will you call again in three days' time? I think the whole thing will be quite satisfactorily cleared up by then.'

'Are you joking, Mr Parker Pyne?'

'I never joke on professional matters, my dear sir. It would occasion distrust in my clients. Shall we say Friday at 11.30? Thank you.'

Evan entered Mr Parker Pyne's office on the Friday morning in a considerable turmoil. Hope and scepticism fought for mastery.

Mr Parker Pyne rose to meet him with a beaming smile.

'Good morning, Mr Llewellyn. Sit down. Have a cigarette?'

Llewellyn waved aside the proffered box.

'Well?' he said.

'Very well indeed,' said Mr Parker Pyne. 'The police arrested the gang last night.'

'The gang? What gang?'

'The Amalfi gang. I thought of them at once when you told me your story. I recognised their methods and once you had described the guests, well, there was no doubt at all in my mind.'

'Who are the Amalfi gang?'

'Father, son and daughter-in-law—that is, if Pietro and Maria are really married—which some doubt.'

'I don't understand.'

'It's quite simple. The name is Italian and no doubt the origin is Italian, but old Amalfi was born in America. His methods are usually the same. He impersonates a real business man, introduces himself to some prominent figure in the jewel business in some European country and then plays his little trick. In this case he was deliberately on the track of the Morning Star. Pointz's idiosyncrasy was well known in the trade. Maria Amalfi played the part of his daughter (amazing creature, twenty-seven at least, and nearly always plays a part of sixteen).'

'Not Eve!' gasped Llewellyn.

'Exactly. The third member of the gang got himself taken on as an extra waiter at the Royal George—it was holiday time, remember, and they would need extra staff. He may even have bribed a regular man to stay away. The scene is set. Eve challenges old Pointz and he takes on the bet. He passes round the diamond as he had done the night before. The waiters enter the room and Leathern retains the stone until they have left the room. When they do leave, the diamond leaves also, neatly attached with a morsel of chewing gum to the underside of the plate that Pietro bears away. So simple!'

'But I *saw* it after that.'

'No, no, you saw a paste replica, good enough to deceive a casual glance. Stein, you told me, hardly looked at it. Eve drops it, sweeps off a glass too and steps firmly on stone and glass together. Miraculous disappearance of diamond. Both Eve and Leathern can submit to as much searching as anyone pleases.'

'Well—I'm—' Evan shook his head, at a loss for words.

'You say you recognised the gang from my description. Had they worked this trick before?'

'Not exactly—but it was their kind of business. Naturally my attention was at once directed to the girl Eve.'

'Why? I didn't suspect her—nobody did. She seemed such a—such a *child*.'

'That is the peculiar genius of Maria Amalfi. She is more like a child than any child possibly could be! And then the plasticine! This bet was supposed to have arisen quite spontaneously—yet the little lady had some plasticine with her all handy. That spoke of premeditation. My suspicions fastened on her at once.'

Llewellyn rose to his feet.

'Well, Mr Parker Pyne, I'm no end obliged to you.'

'Classification,' murmured Mr Parker Pyne. 'The classification of criminal types—it interests me.'

'You'll let me know how much—er—'

'My fee will be quite moderate,' said Mr Parker Pyne. 'It will not make too big a hole in the—er—horse-racing profits. All the same, young man, I should, I think, leave the horses alone in future. Very uncertain animal, the horse.'

'That's all right,' said Evan.

He shook Mr Parker Pyne by the hand and strode from the office.

He hailed a taxi and gave the address of Janet Rustington's flat.

He felt in a mood to carry all before him.

COLIN WILSON

Discovering Cornwall

Colin Wilson, who established his name with *The Outsider* (1956),
and who has since been one of the most versatile and prolific of
writers, describes how he settled in Cornwall.

In the summer of 1954 I was sleeping rough in London—mostly on
Hampstead Heath, and spending my days in the British Museum
reading room, writing my first novel, *Ritual in the Dark*. Possibly
this sounds romantic; in fact it was pretty wearing to the nerves.
And in mid-July, when my girl-friend Joy (now my wife) received
a fortnight's holiday from the library where she worked, my one
thought was to get as far out of London as possible. Neither of us
had been in Cornwall. So we sent our bikes on to Plymouth by
rail, and set out to hitch-hike from London. We stuck to the coast
road—Southampton, Poole, Bridport—and I remember that it was
in Lyme Regis, climbing that steep hill out of the town, looking at
the seagulls nesting on the cliffs, that the weight of oppression
suddenly slipped from my shoulders, and I experienced a sense of
'newness', sheer delight.

I should explain that I am a Midlander; I was born in Leicester,
and spent most of my life there until I moved to London at twenty.
But I am no lover of industrial landscape, or provincial towns.
During my teens I spent a great deal of time cycling around
Leicestershire, Warwickshire, Derbyshire. I had even cycled to the
Lake District. But none of this quite prepared me for the West

Country. I had seen pictures of Devon and Cornwall fishing villages; but they had seemed as remote as Hong Kong or Tahiti. I suppose what astonished me, and shook me into wakefulness, was their accessibility. It seemed amazing that you could get there so easily, without even the train fare in your pocket. I kept thinking: 'Why didn't I do this before?' At seventeen, you suspect that life is going to be an endless series of obstacles and difficulties. The problem of a career—of how you are going to make a living for the next sixty years or so—hangs over you like some symbolic taskmaster with a whip. And it seems that the possibilities you dreamed about in childhood—travel, adventure, fame—are as remote from real life as a Walt Disney movie. I was inclined to agree with Axel who calls the world 'an old slave . . . who promises us the keys to a palace of enchantment, when it clutches only a handful of ashes in its clenched black fist'. So when I first saw the West Country, I was inclined to be suspicious, believing that there must be a catch in it somewhere.

We sat on the quay at Paignton, and ate bananas with Devon cream, and looked at the boats in the harbour, and the fishermen who were obviously real, and not made-up for a pantomime, and again I experienced the sense of freedom, and the suspicion that there had to be a catch in it somewhere. There was: the bananas and cream made me feel sick; but that didn't last long, and the scenery was still there when the sickness passed away.

We drank cider in a pub and had our water-bottles filled up with it. The landlord said in a friendly manner, 'Ah, that'll rot your socks off.' It didn't quite do that, but it acquired a most peculiar tang from the metal of the army water-bottles and tasted like paint-thinner when we tried to drink it for breakfast the next morning. We poured it on the stiff, blue-green grass at the edge of Dartmoor, and I swear that this had begun to wilt when we left an hour later . . .

Joy had a pocket-size copy of Arthur Norway's *Highways and Byways in Devon and Cornwall*, and we took turns in reading it aloud. The style is somewhat flowery: 'To all West Countrymen [Exeter] is a mother city, one who during untold centuries has been their head and capital, and fought their battles and suffered with them when the luck was bad.' In London I would have been very sniffy about this kind of prose; my ideal was the unemotional precision of Eliot, the flat statement of Hemingway. How the hell could a city fight your battles and suffer with you? But in the West Country it became part of the enchantment. I could understand why this particular volume of the *Highways and Byways* series has more myths and fairy tales than any other.

I apologise if this sounds self-indulgently nostalgic. The experience of freedom, of widening horizons, makes an impression that lasts a lifetime, and I would be untrue to the experience if I merely described our itinerary.

In Plymouth we collected the bikes and some camping equipment and the going became heavier. If I had known about the steepness of West Country hills, I would have brought rubber-soled shoes; the steel-studded things I was wearing kept slipping backwards as I pushed the overloaded bicycle up one-in-four gradients, and Joy complained that my language spoilt the scenery. It was definitely a mistake to bring bicycles. But in the evenings when we had set up the tent, and unloaded the primus stove and cooking pots, it was a delight to free-wheel down steep hills, with the odd sensation that the bicycles had become weightless and were about to take off like aeroplanes.

What do I remember clearly about that holiday? I remember camping above Looe, and going to see a film called (I think) *The Knave of Hearts* in a kind of hall in Polperro. This was before the death of Gerard Philippe, and I remember being amazed by his sheer lightness of touch, a champagne-like quality in the comedy that reinforced the mood of the holiday. (His death struck me as a greater tragedy than that of James Dean or Marilyn Monroe.) I remember camping in a field near Gorran churchtown, only a few hundred yards from where we now live, and cycling down to Mevagissey, thinking that the main square, with its lighted shops, looked exactly like a stage set—and a particularly unreal one at that. The next morning the heat of the sun exploded the front tyre on my bike, but I was able to buy a replacement at Ernie Liddicoat's garage on the corner, although it seemed a pity to waste money on this kind of thing when it could be spent on fish and chips and cider. (By this time I had acquired a taste for the vinegary Devon cider, and was upset to find that most of the Cornish pubs stocked only the bottled variety.) I remember the exhilaration of the stiff breeze on the St Mawes sea-front, and of travelling over to Falmouth on the ferry, watching the sunlight on the choppy water. I remember walking too close to a rough sea at St Ives, and getting soaked from head to foot by a large wave, and then running, shivering, back to the camp on the cliff to change. I also recall being disappointed by Hell's Mouth which didn't strike me as nearly spectacular enough after all the other Cornish cliffs.

What impressed me most about Cornwall? The jagged rocks in the sea, and the pleasantness of its pubs. After living in a town all my life, the sheer quantity of fine scenery seemed excessive. And having got used to town pubs, with their large rooms and juke boxes and tarted-up decorations, it was delightful to enter small bars where you had to stoop to avoid the beams, and where it all looked as dark and old as if it hadn't changed in centuries.

But most important, I suppose, was the fact that the trip occurred when it did; at a time when I'd determined to become a writer or bust. If it had happened six years earlier, when I was seventeen, and working in Leicester for the Collector of Taxes, it would only have filled me with an awful nostalgia and dissatisfaction, and become a symbol of all the things I was missing. But it happened when I had already decided that I'd had enough of conventional existence and 'playing it safe'—when I'd determined that I would rather become a tramp or a monk than spend my life doing an ordinary job. I felt I'd cut my cables, and there was no return. (I even remember telling Joy, as we cycled through Par, that she shouldn't regard our relationship as too permanent, because one day I'd probably end in a monastery.) And Cornwall seemed like a kind of advance payment of freedom, a confirmation of the decision to cut loose.

Subsequent visits reinforced this mood. We returned the following year, this time without bicycles. Since my last trip I had moved indoors again—to a room in New Cross— and written most of a book called *The Outsider*. Some time around March 1955 I submitted a dozen or so pages of this book to the publisher Victor Gollancz, and he replied almost immediately that he would be interested in publishing it. Shortly before we set out for Cornwall, I sent Gollancz about half the typescript. He replied that he would definitely publish it, and took me out to lunch. When we took a holiday in Cornwall I still had one chapter to write, and I had that excited, slightly sick feeling that children have on Christmas Eve. Now that the book would definitely be published, I could think at last in terms of a career—a real career. The next stage was to finish my novel, *Ritual in the Dark*, and then write a sequel to *The Outsider* about religious mystics. The butterflies-in-the-stomach feeling sprang out of a sort of fear: the feeling that I had so much to say, so much work ahead of me . . . and that there could still be a slip between cup and the lip. Perhaps Gollancz wouldn't like the second half of the book, and would decide not to publish after all . . . But drinking again in the low-beamed Cornish pubs, and scrambling across rocks at the edge of the sea, I couldn't really believe anything could go wrong.

I was correct. My assumption of the immediate fame that would follow publication was sheer inexperience, but it happened. *The Outsider* came out (in May 1956) at a time when the literary scene had been quiescent for a year or so. Dylan Thomas had died three years earlier, and his death had seemed to mark the end of the 'apocalyptic' era— of Isherwood's Berlin novels and the poems of Auden and Spender, and Ronald Duncan's *This Way to the Tomb*. And although a few new talents had appeared in the early fifties—Kingsley Amis, John Wain, Iris Murdoch, Angus Wilson— there was still no sign of a 'generation', a group of writers with a general direction. I suppose *The Outsider* and Osborne's *Look Back in Anger* (which appeared earlier the same month) appeared to be 'landmarks' in the same sense as *The Waste Land* or *Ulysses*. (I certainly thought of *The Outsider* as my own *Waste Land*.) Whatever the reason, I had more than a successful book on my hands. I also had a reputation as some sort of figurehead of a new generation. For a few months it looked as if Osborne and myself had achieved, in one single step, the kind of dominant position that other writers had achieved only after several books.

So when Joy and I returned to the West Country in July 1956, we were in a different position from previous years. To begin with, there was enough money to eat restaurant meals and also enough to take ourselves—and our bikes—on trains when we got tired of pedalling. This time we drove down to Devon in style, sharing a sports car (or at least the cost of the petrol) with Ken Allsop and Dan Farson. We stayed for a couple of days with Dan's father, Negley (author of *Way of a Transgressor*) and met Henry William-

son and Negley's next-door neighbour, Malcolm Elwin (whose
First Romantics was one of my favourite books). All this was
a little breathtaking—to mix with authors, to be praised by
critics, to be written about in magazines and newspapers. I didn't
entirely like it. I'm a retiring sort of person, basically rather shy.
Being approved of so much was a strain, like walking on a tight-
rope. I would have been happier if the book had simply made me a
reputation as an 'interesting' writer, worth watching. For an
introvert the best-seller status was unnerving. I felt like that little
soldier in Akutagawa's *Yam Gruel* who always dreams of being able
to eat his fill of yam gruel—until a rich samurai with a sense of
humour invites him to his house, and then places vast tureens of
yam gruel in front of him. (Naturally, he just feels sick.)

So this time the West Country was simply a tonic for the nerves,
and I can remember nothing about that trip, except that the porter
failed to unload our bikes at the Launceston railway station, and
we had to spend the night camping in a nearby field, waiting for
them to be sent back from Penzance . . .

And that might well have been the end of my relationship with
the West Country—except for occasional holidays—if it was not
for chance. My mistrust of overnight fame proved justified.
As the success rolled on like some giant snowball and *The Outsider*
went through impression after impression, people naturally began
to ask if I was really all that brilliant and original, and if I deserved
quite so much publicity and praise. England's 'intellectual establish-
ment' felt they had been stampeded, and people who had never
joined in the praise took the opportunity to say they'd never considered the book much good anyway. By Christmas it seemed that
every critic in England was waiting to admit that the whole thing
had been an absurd mistake. I was utterly and totally 'discredited', as
if I'd been a confidence swindler who had been publicly exposed.
There was still plenty of publicity, but now it was uniformly
hostile. Victor Gollancz, who had sold 40,000 copies of the book—
as well as selling it to America and a dozen foreign publishers—
saw his investment dwindling. He advised me to take a job and
spend five years writing my next book. When I showed no sign
of accepting this advice, he suggested that I move to a cottage in
the country and try to keep out of the newspapers.

Early in 1957, sick of the atmosphere of hostility in London, I decided to try out his suggestion. I rented a room in a huge old house near Totnes which belonged to Hugh Heckstall Smith, a retired headmaster, but it was lonely without Joy. I returned to London, and more publicity. A poet living in the same house in Notting Hill Gate asked me if I'd be interested in renting his cottage near Mevagissey. One weekend in early March we travelled down by train and spent the evening at a guest-house owned by D.S. Savage, the literary critic, in Mevagissey. The next morning a taxi drove us out through Portmellon, up the incredibly steep hill that we had free-wheeled down three years earlier (Bodrugan) and on to the farm at the top of the hill. Down a long, muddy track we found the cottage, with white cob walls that were nearly a yard thick, and a corrugated tin roof painted blue. It had four rooms—two up and two down—and a bathroom with an ancient boiler. If you stood in the bedrooms, you could see the rooms below through cracks in the floor-boards. There was no electricity —it was too far off the main road—and drinking water came from a well in the garden. The cottage was at the bottom of a green valley which led down to the sea. A noisy stream flowed near the front door so that it always sounded as if it were raining heavily. And there were even some flowers growing on the trellis round the door, although (not being much of a countryman) I can't recall what they were. The rent was thirty shillings a week, which was also a consideration. I had already spent most of the royalties from *The Outsider*. We decided immediately to take it, on a two-year lease. A couple of weeks later we hired a van, packed all our belongings in it, and drove down from London.

It ought to have been idyllic—the country existence. The spring that year was superb. The scenery was magnificent for walking; the great cliffs between Portmellon and Gorran Haven, with the isolated beach at Chapel Point. We bought an old car, for £40, so Mevagissey became easily accessible. When this contraption exploded after a few months, we bought a new Anglia and started to explore Cornwall. I certainly had no regrets about leaving London and the 'literary scene' with its empty-headedness and bitchery. But the experience of the past year had been too vertiginous, and I was suffering from a kind of moral hangover. Three years earlier I had been in Mevagissey, dreaming about literary fame. Now it had arrived—and gone. So the quiet had an ominous quality, as if this were the place where I had been left by a receding tide.

Fortunately, I am a recluse by nature. It took me about six months to get accustomed to the amazing quiet of the countryside; then I began to appreciate it. In New Cross I had lived above a railway line, and after the first night the trains made no difference at all. Silence was at first more difficult to get used to. And the aloneness. Sometimes whole days passed without our seeing anyone. At night there were grasshoppers chirping around the cottage and an owl in the tree outside the kitchen window. Moths fluttered against the windows and got burnt against the chimneys of the Aladdin lamps. (I had installed an electric generator—in order to run the gramophone—but the batteries were so poor that we tried not to use electric light.)

You could follow the brook down to the valley, over three or four fields to the sea. Colona Beach was usually covered with pools of cow dung and masses of drying seaweed. Part of it was 'private', belonging to the houses at Chapel Point. The story has it that these houses were built by an enterprising architect a few decades ago, but that no one wanted to live in such a remote spot. He commited suicide; then, one by one, the white Mediterranean-style houses were bought at enormous prices, so they are now our local equivalent of Millionaires' Row.

If you turn right at the beach, and walk uphill towards Gorran Haven, you see some of the finest cliff scenery in southern Cornwall. There are long sheer drops down to the sea, and the usual jagged rocks pointing up at you. One of these rocks, as big as a large house, stands in a hollow in the cliff-face; this is Bodrugan's Leap, from which the farm takes its name. According to the guide-books, Bodrugan was a supporter of Richard III, and after the battle of Bosworth Field he was ordered by Henry VII to be deprived of his lands. Richard Edgcumbe, of Cotehele, his old enemy, came to arrest him at his castle at Bodrugan, and pursued him on horseback towards the cliff edge. Bodrugan spurred his horse over the cliff and on to the great rock below— killing the horse—and then swam out to one of his own boats that conveyed him to France and safety.

Another mile along these cliffs brings you to a point from which you can see Gorran Haven, a small fishing village (where I now live). Like Mevagissey, it is surrounded by hills and cliffs so that it looks almost too picturesque to be true. I can remember my first walk from Old Walls to Gorran Haven on the first day we came to look at the cottage. Our nominal 'landlord', the poet Louis Adeane, was with us. (He rented the cottage; financial necessity finally drove him to take a job in London, but he continued to rent the place, dreaming of the day when he would have enough money to return. He never did.) On a bright spring morning I found all this so magical that I could hardly believe my luck. I kept thinking that he was sure to change his mind, now he had seen it again, and decide to return himself . . . And during the two years we lived in Old Walls I never felt wholly secure, for I could not imagine how anyone could continue to live in London when, with some slight sacrifice of comfort, he could be in this superb place. It was this feeling of insecurity, as well as the need to find a larger place to house my increasing collection of books and records, that led us to look round for a house in 1958. We found one outside Gorran Haven, built only a few years earlier by a retired couple. They had found the loneliness more than they had bargained for and wanted to get back to the Home Counties. And so we took the next step in acquiring Cornish 'nationality' by becoming the owners of a house with two acres of land, a step that would have struck me as inconceivable in 1954.

If you walk down to Gorran Haven and continue along the cliff path, you have to walk waist-deep in ferns for a quarter of a mile and you find yourself on another beach, Vault, one of the longest in this part of the world. Because it is so inaccessible that it is impossible to drive a car closer than a quarter of a mile away, this remains fairly deserted; even in the height of the tourist season, there are seldom more than a few dozen people along its enormous length. And if you care to plod over its yielding pebbles to the far end, you can reckon on total solitude, beyond the reach of the noisiest transistor radio.

I wish to avoid sounding like a guide-book, but since this is one of my favourite walks, perhaps I might indulge myself a little further. Assuming you do not want to spend the day on the beach, you can turn right up the hill just before you reach it and emerge, after a steep climb over a couple of fields, at Lamledra Farm (now a riding-stable). It is now possible to continue to

follow the shore-line along a narrow asphalted road (with a few
farm gates to open) above Vault beach. Headlands stick out on
both sides. The magnificent, gorse-covered promontory on the
right is the Dodman, an ominous-sounding name which actually
means a snail. You can walk right out to the point of the Dodman,
if you don't mind some rough going, to the great stone memorial
cross which overlooks the sea. We walked out there one dark
afternoon and watched a sudden storm blow up. The winds were
so high, and the downpour so violent, that we decided to forgo
the pleasure of watching the turmoil from the cliff-top and hurried
back to the Land-Rover parked half a mile away. This was a pity.
At exactly the time we were on our way back, a boat called the
Darlwin, full of holiday-makers, vanished off the Dodman.
Against the advice of the harbour-master, she had decided to set
out from Fowey to return to Falmouth. She was seen off
Mevagissey before the storm, then she simply vanished. What
happened, I am fairly sure, is that the bottom of the boat caved in
suddenly when she hit a high wave, and she went down like a
stone, taking forty passengers, many of them women and children,
with her. The boat has never been found, neither have the bodies
which are probably trapped inside. If we had stayed on the
Dodman for ten minutes longer, I might have been able to pin-
point the spot where she disappeared.

Beyond the Dodman, walking enthusiasts can still continue for
another mile or so before they encounter (at Boswinger) the coast
road leading to Caerhays and Veryan. In fact, at the bottom of
a steep, winding hill, down a road wide enough for only one car,
they will discover one of the pleasantest beaches in the area,
Hemmick. Because of its enormous rocks—with narrow passage-
ways between them—Hemmick has a fairy-tale quality, and
children love it. I always go down there after the first storm of the
winter, and load up the Land-Rover with driftwood; there is
usually enough to last me as kindling throughout the winter, and
some of the great heavy spars can be sawn up into logs that burn
with a pale blue flame.

Because Cornwall has been such an enormous part of my life,
because I have lived here and brought up children here, I suppose
it has entered into my bloodstream. Fate was kind in directing
me in 1957. For nearly a decade it remained the peaceful, in-

efficient, shabby, unexploited place it had been for centuries, and I saw the last of this. It is still a highly attractive county, not too crowded, hardly commercialised at all compared to Blackpool or Brighton, but the twentieth century has definitely arrived. Perhaps in another ten years I shall feel sufficiently detached to write about the Cornwall I knew when I first came here . . .

Acknowledgements

The Editor and Publishers are most grateful to the following (publishers included are the original ones unless otherwise indicated):

H.R.H. The Prince of Wales for his Foreword, Sir John Betjeman for his poem 'Exeter' (John Murray); Dr Charles Causley for his poem 'Launceston Castle', written especially for *The West Country Book*; Dame Daphne du Maurier for the extract from her book *Vanishing Cornwall* (Gollancz); Agatha Christie Limited for 'The Regatta Mystery' (Collins) by Dame Agatha Christie; John Fowles for the extract from his novel *The French Lieutenant's Woman* (Jonathan Cape); Christopher Fry for his essay, written especially for *The West Country Book*; Winston Graham for 'Jud's Funeral' from his novel *Jeremy Poldark* (T. Werner Laurie and Bodley Head); Professor W. G. Hoskins for the extract from his book *Devon* (Collins); Laurie Lee for 'Winter and Summer' from *Cider with Rosie* (Hogarth Press); Freda Hastings and Laurie Lee for Frank Mansell's poem 'Stone Wall' from *Cotswold Ballads* (Wittantree Press, 1969); Eileen O'Casey and Messrs Macmillan for 'Deep in Devon' from Sean O'Casey's *Sunset and Evening Star* (Macmillan); Miss P. V. Pitman whose original tinted etching of St Lawrence Church, High Street, Exeter, is lent by kind permission from the collection in the Royal Albert Memorial Museum, Exeter; Adelaide Ross and the Royal Literary Fund for 'Widecombe Concert' from Eden Phillpotts's novel *Widecombe Fair* (John Murray); Foy Quiller-Couch for Sir Arthur Quiller-Couch's story 'The Roll-Call of the Reef' from *Wandering Heath* (J.M. Dent, 1928); Dr A.L. Rowse for his story 'St Carroc's Crucifix', written especially for *The West Country Book*; Derek Tangye for the extract from *A Gull on the Roof* (Michael Joseph); Wynford Vaughan-Thomas and the Literary Executors of Dylan Thomas for 'The Crumbs of One Man's Year' from *Quite Early One Morning* (J.M. Dent); Auberon Waugh for the extract from Evelyn Waugh's novel *Scoop* (Chapman and Hall); Richard Williamson for the extract from Henry Williamson's novel *The Pathway* (Faber and Faber); and Colin Wilson for 'Discovering Cornwall'.

Picture Credits

J. Allen Cash: 33, 39 (below), 90; Colour Library International: 95 (below); Dawlish Town Council (Michael S. Alexander): 92 (below); Michael Hales: 35, 94 (above); Liverpool University: 36/7; Roger Mayne: 92 (above); National Gallery (E. T. Archive Ltd): 91 (below); Plymouth City Art Gallery: 34 (above); Royal Albert Memorial Museum, Exeter: 91 (above); Victoria and Albert Museum: jacket, 94 (below).